DEBT CONVERSION IN LATIN AMERICA: PANACEA OR PANDEMIC?

POLICY ESSAY NO. 2

DEBT CONVERSION
IN LATIN AMERICA:

PANACEA OR PANDEMIC?

MARY L. WILLIAMSON

SERIES EDITOR: RICHARD E. FEINBERG

OVERSEAS DEVELOPMENT COUNCIL
WASHINGTON, DC

ISBN: 1-56517-001-6
Printed in the United States of America.

Director of Publication: Christine E. Contee
Editor: Jacqueline Edlund-Braun
Cover and book design by Tim Kenney Design, Inc.

Contents

Foreword

Most Latin American countries have experimented with various debt conversion programs. *Debt Conversion in Latin America: Pandemic or Panacea?* examines the experiences of Chile, Argentina, Brazil, and Mexico, focusing on the specific macroeconomic context and policy priorities behind each program and the costs and benefits of different strategies. The author concludes that debt conversion is neither the cure nor the curse that some observors have claimed, and she extracts from the case studies lessons for debtors to maximize their benefits.

This analysis is the second in ODC's *Policy Essay* series that provides a forum for authors to express opinions, make predictions, and assess policy ramifications in the field of U.S.-Third World relations. The relatively abbreviated format is short enough to serve as a digestible brief for policy-related application, while lengthy enough to allow room for more extended analysis.

Debt Conversion in Latin America: Pandemic or Panacea? is the latest in ODC's considerable body of work on the international debt crisis and the respective roles of borrowers and lenders, including commercial banks, governments, and international financial institutions. Highlights of these ODC studies include *Uncertain Future: Commercial Banks in the Third World* (1985), *Between Two Worlds: The World Bank's Next Decade* (1986), and *Pulling Together: The International Monetary Fund in a Multipolar World* (1989).

The Overseas Development Council gratefully acknowledges the support of The Ford Foundation, The Rockefeller Foundation, and The William and Flora Hewlett Foundation for the Council's overall program.

John W. Sewell
President
November 1991

Acknowledgments

Many people have generously assisted in the preparation of this essay. In particular, I would like to thank Richard Feinberg, Executive Vice President and Director of Studies of the Overseas Development Council; the staff of the *Stanford Journal of International Law;* the staff of the United Nations Economic Commission for Latin America/Centre on Transnational Enterprises Joint Unit, Santiago, Chile; the Latin American Studies Department at the Johns Hopkins School of Advanced International Studies, which awarded me a grant to carry out this research; and The Andrew W. Mellon Foundation, which funded that grant. Special thanks are also due to Melissa Vaughn for her helpful comments and editing. This essay is based on an earlier version in the *Stanford Journal of International Law,* Vol. 27, No. 2, 1991.

Executive Summary

Some observers hail debt conversion as the salvation of Latin American debtor countries, but other experts warn that debt conversion is a deceptive and dangerous debt management tool. Yet another school of thought holds that this debate is quickly growing irrelevant, because debt conversion is rapidly being eclipsed by other strategies for reengagement with the international financial system.

This essay argues that debt conversion remains an important element of external debt management in several of the largest Latin American debtor countries, although conversion programs have a limited life span and may have worked themselves out of a job in certain countries, notably Chile. It concludes that because Latin American debt conversion strategies vary considerably in their policy content and macroeconomic underpinnings, assessments of their costs and benefits must be made on a country-by-country basis, in a way that addresses differing goals and contexts.

Four countries' experiments with debt conversion provide the focus for this essay. The case of Chile is presented in particular detail to illustrate the regulatory and financial issues surrounding debt conversion policy, the trade-offs implicit in designing a program, and the life cycle of a mature debt conversion program. The essay also analyzes the cases of Argentina, Brazil, and Mexico, which illustrate the diverse roles that debt conversion can play in shaping debt negotiation and economic reform strategies.

As the Chilean case study highlights, large-scale debt reduction is only one possible priority for a debt conversion program. Other countries, notably Brazil and Mexico, have emphasized more selective policies that attempt to use the debt conversion subsidy to attract particularly desirable types of foreign investment. The trade-off between the quantity and quality of debt conversions has sparked considerable debate in each of the countries studied, and it underscores the inherent limitations of the debt conversion tool.

At times, large-scale debt conversion may not be a realistic option. Debt conversions feed inflation and exacerbate capital flight if they occur in an unstable macroeconomic environment or if a country's capital market cannot absorb long-term bonds to offset the monetary effects of conversion. Even in Chile, where sterilization measures successfully dampened the impact of rapid debt conversion, the conversion program added to pressures on the capital and foreign exchange markets. The policy that Argentina is now pursuing—and which Brazil may soon implement as well—is to link debt conversions to privatizations and thereby avoid monetary expansion despite the absence of a solid long-term capital market. This approach may enable debtor countries to convert large sums of foreign debt without overloading still-fragile stabilization programs.

In addition to supporting privatization efforts, debt conversion programs can mesh with other elements of economic restructuring. For example, Chile's program has enhanced the confidence of foreign and domestic investors, strengthened the balance sheets of existing domestic enterprises, and promoted exports. Furthermore, debt conversion policies are often a bargaining chip in negotiations with foreign creditors and can thus produce debt reduction indirectly as well as directly. Argentina and Brazil are both pursuing Brady Plan agreements to scale back their foreign debt, and one issue their creditors will no doubt raise in upcoming negotiations will be the relative generosity and scale of their current or prospective debt conversion programs.

No other Latin American country has emulated Chile by placing debt conversion at the center of its debt reduction strategy. In part, this is a result of creditors' recent willingness to provide debt relief beyond that available through debt conversion. However, debtor countries also recognize that conversions entail costs, including implicit subsidization of selected private investments, the generation of unknown future foreign exchange outflows, and destabilizing pressure on inflation and exchange rates. These expenses and risks rise sharply when the underlying economy is not sufficiently stable to absorb the pressures generated by debt conversion, and in such a situation conversions can reduce rather than increase overall investor confidence.

No single bottom line summarizes the costs and benefits of debt conversion in Latin America. Each country should seek to identify debt conversion policies that build on its economic adjustment strategy and that can adapt to changing market conditions and negotiating possibilities. This essay suggests that there is wide scope for innovative design and management of conversion programs and that such policies continue to represent a promising debt management option for many Latin American debtor countries.

Part I
Latin America's Continuing Experiments with Debt Conversion

LATIN AMERICA'S CONTINUING EXPERIMENTS WITH DEBT CONVERSION

■ IN THE LATE 1980S, THE INTERNATIONAL financial community hailed debt conversion as a vital tool for overcoming the Latin American debt crisis. Creditors pressed governments to formalize and expand the avenues by which they could transform their loan portfolios into equities or cash. Domestic and foreign investors favored the subsidies afforded by debt conversions, and debtor governments were often tempted by the prospect of repaying their debts at a rate dictated by secondary market forces rather than their loan documents. Debt conversion programs became a featured attraction on the debt management "menus" negotiated between borrowers and lenders.

Debt conversion is no longer such a prominent element in debt management strategies. Chile's much-heralded debt conversion program has slowed to a crawl, and a plethora of new debt reduction techniques and structural adjustment measures in major debtor countries has captured center stage. Surveying the present landscape, one might think that debt conversion programs were in a state of permanent decline.[1] However, Argentina has assigned a new and important role to foreign debt conversions in its economic planning, and Brazil is at least contemplating a debt conversion initiative. Mexico has also sporadically sponsored debt conversions, although its various conversion programs have never been central to its structural adjustment or debt reduction efforts. Past and present programs in these countries demonstrate the wide range of functions that debt conversions can serve and suggest that debt conversions will contribute significantly to economic management in Latin America for the next several years.

This essay analyzes in detail the pioneering debt conversion program in Chile to illuminate the model to which many other national programs compare themselves. It also reviews conversion programs in Argentina, Brazil, and Mexico, outlining the various types of debt conversions that these countries have authorized and examining their programs' contrasting objectives. Essentially, the designers of a debt conversion program must choose among three competing but not mutually exclusive goals: achieving a heavy volume of debt reduction, encouraging additional high-priority investments, and capturing a large proportion of the secondary market discount. Debtor-country governments can also choose to pursue these goals through other means, such as negotiated debt relief, informal debt conversions, and structural reforms to promote private investment. This essay explores the role that debt conversions can play in debt management and structural adjustment efforts in Latin America and identifies alternative policy combinations that can achieve equivalent effects.

The following section analyzes the content and evolution of Chile's debt conversion policies in considerable detail to illustrate the relevant regulatory and financial issues and the motivations behind specific policy choices. This discussion highlights the trade-offs implicit in emphasizing one or another paradigm for debt conversions. The third section of this essay presents the history and results of experiments with debt conversions in Argentina, Brazil, and Mexico, thus illustrating a wide range of alternative approaches and their costs and benefits.

These four debt conversion portraits emphasize the specific macroeconomic setting and policy priorities behind each program. Divergent debt management strategies and foreign investment patterns, along with the varying pace and design of structural adjustment efforts among Latin American debtors, have given debt conversions a different hue in each country. For example, Chile's liberal regulations have encouraged a broad array of conversions that has anchored debt management efforts and revived private investment levels, whereas Mexico has permitted conversions only under strict supervision and does not rely on them for debt management or investment promotion. Furthermore, each of the four debtor countries has implemented a succession of debt conversion policies in response to shifting national priorities, financial market pressures, and macroeconomic circumstances. Such a flexible approach to debt conversion enables countries to adjust to these dynamic factors albeit at the cost of creating an aura of policy instability around many debt conversion programs.

Conversion policies can be a useful bargaining chip in negotiations between debtors and commercial banks. At the same time, conversions can help prepare a country for successful debt negotiations by financing privatization programs and contributing to other structural adjustment efforts that creditors demand as prerequisites to debt relief. However, as the country studies suggest, the potential gains from and costs of debt conversion programs are significant and are shaped by regulatory choices, so that debtor-country governments should not select a debt conversion strategy with solely their bargaining positions vis-à-vis creditors in mind. Instead, they should determine how they can harness conversions to achieve desirable goals such as a financially stronger private sector and an improving trade balance, while minimizing potential risks such as rising inflation and future drains on foreign exchange reserves.

A final open question raised by these country studies is how changing global economic conditions will alter the lessons taught by past experiences with debt conversion. The global contraction in credit and the rapidly growing roster of countries trying to lure foreign investment to bolster economic reforms do not augur well for the future success of Latin American debt conversion programs, because they heighten competition for scarce investment capital. On the other hand, Mexico and Argentina have recently succeeded in attracting substantial investments through debt conversions despite the gloomy world economic climate. Thus, on balance, optimism is warranted. Other Latin American debtors may not relive the Cinderella story of the Chilean economy during the 1980s, but the hard work and sacrifices involved in structural adjustments may still earn a high yield, some of which can be reaped through debt conversions.

Part II
Debt Conversion
in Chile

DEBT CONVERSION IN CHILE

■   CHILE WAS ONE OF THE FIRST COUNTRIES to introduce a formal debt conversion scheme in the wake of the 1982 debt crisis. Its conversion program is notable for both its longevity and the large portion of the nation's external debt converted under its auspices. The country's open business climate and permissive debt conversion norms have fueled an especially rapid drop in the private sector's foreign debt and have contributed to a far-reaching privatization initiative. The flexibility of this program has also facilitated an unusually wide range of debt conversion transactions in response to market demand for varying types of conversions. At the same time, Chile's debt conversion policies have generated much controversy, and the Aylwin government introduced important changes in the program upon taking office in 1990.

CHILE'S FOREIGN DEBT CRISIS

■   CHILE PARTICIPATED ENTHUSIASTICALLY in the foreign borrowing boom of the late 1970s.[2] Its total external debt soared from less than $5 billion in 1976 to over $17 billion by 1982, by which time Chile's stock of debt totaled 68 percent of GDP.[3] Private sector borrowers held the majority of Chilean debt (see Table 1), in contrast to the situation in most other highly indebted Latin American countries. Furthermore, government guarantees covered less than 1 percent of the private debt, reflecting the official policy of reducing the public sector's role in the economy and permitting market forces to operate unfettered. However, government policy remained an important stimulus to private sector behavior. Progressive overvaluation of the exchange rate after 1978—a side effect of the government's anti-inflation program—encouraged heavy foreign borrowing, and deregulation of international capital flows further fueled the debt boom.[4]

TABLE 1. MEDIUM- AND LONG-TERM EXTERNAL DEBT IN CHILE, 1980-1990

($U.S. billions)

	1980	1981	1982	1983	1984	1985	1986	1987	1988	1989	1990
Total	9.4	12.6	13.8	14.8	17.0	17.7	17.8	17.2	15.5	13.3	14.1
Public Sector	4.7	4.4	5.2	8.1	10.6	12.5	14.4	14.7	13.1	10.1	9.3
(of which guaranteed private sector debts)	0.1	0.1	(0.6)	(1.5)	(1.7)	(2.0)	(2.9)	(2.7)	(2.1)	(1.1)	(0.6)
Private Sector	4.7	8.1	8.7	6.7	6.4	5.1	3.4	2.5	2.4	3.1	4.7

Note: Figures are for December 31 of each year. 1990 figures are preliminary.

Sources: Chilean External Debt 1988 *(Santiago, Chile: Central Bank of Chile, 1988), p. 25, table 1, and* Boletín Mensual, *No. 755, Jan. 1991, p. 133.*

Chile's liberal economic climate contributed to international banks' enthusiasm for lending, but the same liberalism exacerbated the initial impact of the 1982 debt crisis.[5] In 1982, Chile's GDP dropped 14.1 percent—the worst performance of any Latin American country in response to the initial shock of the debt crisis—and production dropped a further 0.7 percent in 1983 (see Table 2). With population growth close to 2 percent a year, the per capita economic decline in Chile was even more devastating.

One key factor behind the severity of Chile's initial reaction to the international credit crunch was the structure of its domestic private sector. Production was concentrated in several highly leveraged private conglomerates, whose holdings included important financial institutions as

TABLE 2. MACROECONOMIC INDICATORS FOR CHILE, 1980-1989

($U.S. millions)

	GDP growth *(percentages)*	Investment *(% GDP)*			Real long-term interest rate *(percentages)*	Current account account *(% GDP)*	Inflation rate *(percentages)*
		Total	Private	Public			
1980	7.8	17.6	12.0	5.6	8.4	7.1	31.2
1981	5.5	19.5	14.1	5.4	13.2	14.5	9.5
1982	-14.1	15.0	10.2	4.8	12.1	9.5	20.7
1983	-0.7	12.9	7.7	5.2	7.7	5.7	23.1
1984	6.3	13.2	6.7	6.5	8.4	10.7	23.0
1985	2.4	14.8	7.9	6.9	8.2	8.3	26.4
1986	5.7	15.0	7.8	7.2	4.1	6.5	17.4
1987	5.7	16.5	10.0	6.6	4.2	4.3	21.5
1988	7.4	17.0	11.1	6.0	4.6	0.8	12.7
1989	10.0	20.3	n.a.	n.a.	8.8	3.6	21.4

Sources: 1980-88 figures from Andrés Solimano, "How Private Investment Reacts to Changing Macroeconomic Conditions: The Case of Chile in the 1980s," Working Paper, Policy, Planning and Research Department, World Bank, December 1989, table 1; 1989 figures from Central Bank of Chile.

well as major industrial concerns.[6] Many companies whose debt service capacities had depended on continued access to foreign capital markets collapsed in a wave of bankruptcies beginning in 1982.[7] These failures in turn decimated the domestic banking sector, where loan portfolios were top-heavy with loans to failing companies related to the banks through private conglomerates.

The Chilean government stepped in to salvage the financial sector by closing some banks, nationalizing others, and taking over troubled loans to protect the solvency of the remaining private banks.[8] Thus the collapse of private financial intermediation and investment spurred the public sector to take a more active role in the economy, as confirmed by the steady rise in public investment between 1982 and 1986. However, private investment plunged more than 50 percent between 1981 and 1984, and the public sector's enhanced efforts did not come close to compensating for earlier private investment levels. Total domestic investment dropped from 19.5 percent of GDP in 1981 to a low of 12.9 percent in 1983 and only 13.2 percent in 1984.

Production levels began to recover in 1984, when Chile registered a 6.3 percent rise in GDP. However, the collapse of long-term bank lending to Latin America raised concerns about the sustainability of this growth, because Chile was providing a net capital outflow to foreign creditors rather than investing the full benefit of its savings in future production. The International Monetary Fund and international development banks extended new credits, but the support of these institutions did not approach the volume of interest and amortization outflows to commercial banks.[9]

The government's initial strategy for minimizing this resource drain was to engage in a series of debt restructuring negotiations with bank creditors, through which it succeeded in reducing interest spreads, extending amortization schedules, and obtaining a retiming agreement and a debt buyback authorization.[10] Nonetheless, the cost of foreign debt service remained formidable; Chile spent 63 percent of its export earnings in 1983 on interest and amortization payments, and this figure had

TABLE 3. CHILE'S EXTERNAL DEBT SERVICE, 1980-1989

	1980	1981	1982	1983	1984	1985	1986	1987	1988	1989
					($U.S. billions)					
Total debt service	2.3	3.2	2.9	2.2	2.3	2.1	2.0	1.7	1.7	1.2
Amortization	1.4	1.8	1.2	0.9	0.5	0.4	0.4	0.3	0.6	0.3
Interest	0.9	1.4	1.7	1.3	1.8	1.7	1.6	1.4	1.0	0.9
Exports[a]	6.0	5.0	4.6	4.6	4.5	4.5	5.0	6.3	8.3	8.1
					(percentages)					
Debt service/ exports	38	64	63	48	51	47	40	27	20	15
Interest/exports	15	28	37	28	40	38	32	22	12	11

Note: Figures may not total because of rounding.

[a]1989 export figure includes only exports of goods and is a preliminary estimate; earlier export totals cover both goods and nonfinancial services and thus give a higher base in calculating the debt service.

Sources: Chilean External Debt 1988 (Santiago, Chile: Central Bank of Chile, 1988); Boletín Mensual No. 748, June 1990.

dropped by only 12 percent two years later (Table 3). The new bank loans needed to liberate additional resources for domestic investment proved elusive. In 1983, a commercial bank debt restructuring agreement included $1.3 billion in new long-term loans, in comparison to total interest payments on external debt in that year of $1.7 billion. Later negotiations produced progressively less new money.

Rescheduling agreements between Chile and its commercial bank creditors did lead to a radical restructuring of the country's external obligations, in which the government agreed to guarantee successively higher proportions of the large private financial sector debt.[11] By 1986 the government was responsible, directly or indirectly, for 80 percent of the country's external debt, as compared with a 38 percent share in 1982.

The government's desire to escape the crushing weight of this debt burden coincided with growing commercial bank interest in debt reduction mechanisms. The possibility of relying on debt conversions to reduce foreign debt appeared especially attractive to the Chilean government because conversions could complement an ongoing privatization campaign and promote private foreign investment. The Pinochet government was not dissuaded by the drawbacks of promoting a high volume of debt conversions, which included subsidizing private investment and selling off national assets at depressed prices. As a result, Chile launched a fast-moving and flexible debt conversion program and proved that such conversions could be vital to recovering from excessive foreign indebtedness. However, no other Latin American country has followed Chile by relying on debt conversions as the sole engine of debt reduction, which suggests that the Pinochet government pursued unorthodox priorities and benefited from unusual political circumstances in adopting this debt management strategy.

. . . .

MECHANISMS FOR DEBT CONVERSION

■   CHILE'S INITIAL DEBT CONVERSION PROGRAM, much of which still operates today, encompassed three formal mechanisms: Chapters XVIII and XIX of the Compendium of Foreign Exchange Rules,[12] and Article 1c of Decree Law 600 (D.L. 600), the statute governing foreign investments made through either equity purchases or project loans.[13] Two key variables differentiate debt conversion mechanisms: 1) their limits on the initial conversion of foreign debts into local currency or peso-denominated domestic obligations, and 2) the restrictions they place on investors' use of the local currency or financial instruments obtained through a conversion (see box on the various types of debt conversions).

Central bank statistics on debt conversion track two additional activities not governed by formal regulations: "portfolio exchanges" between foreign and domestic banks, which have played a minor role in debt reduction; and the much larger category of "other" conversions, most of which have involved direct prepayment of loans in local currency

The terms "debt conversion" and "debt swap" encompass a wide range of transactions that vary according to the type of debt being converted, the foreign or domestic entity doing the converting, and the kind of obligation substituting for the converted foreign debt.

In a **DEBT-EQUITY CONVERSION**—probably the best-known type—a foreign-currency-denominated obligation is repaid to its holder in local currency, or with local-currency-denominated instruments, on the condition that the proceeds will be used to purchase equity in some predefined domestic investment project. Such a transaction reduces the outstanding foreign debt of the country involved and usually injects new domestic currency or long-term bonds into the economy. It sometimes creates a new foreign claim on local assets. Chile's Chapter XIX provides framework for debt-equity conversions.

A **DEBT-PESO SWAP** essentially involves the preliminary stages of a debt-equity conversion without the follow-up. An investor buys a country's foreign debt on the secondary market (or decides to convert a debt that it already holds) and negotiates an agreement to exchange this debt for a specified sum of local currency or local-currency-denominated debt. The investor is free to decide how to spend these proceeds: the government's stewardship of a debt-peso conversion extends only to the terms of the redenomination agreement. Chile's Chapter XVIII program institutionalizes debt-peso swaps.

DEBT-FOR-GOODS CONVERSIONS involve the payment of foreign-currency debts in exportable products. These transactions amount to a discounted prepayment of foreign debt, but they may offer countries the side benefit of enlisting commercial bank assistance in promoting nontraditional exports.

DEBT-FOR-CHARITY CONVERSIONS involve redemptions of foreign debts in which the foreign creditors are "paid" by a debtor country's commitment to devote budgetary and management resources, or even new laws and regulations, to a particular cause. For example, the government might pay the local currency equivalent of its debt repayment obligation to an environmental charity, which would then make a desired investment.

In a **DEBT BUYBACK,** a close cousin to a debt conversion, a debtor negotiates an agreement with its bank creditors to prepay some portion of its foreign currency obligations, with the prepayment rate usually being determined through an auction. Such prepayments reduce a country's debt without altering its foreign currency denomination or substituting alternative obligations.

Another relative of debt conversions is the **DEBT/BOND SWAP**, in which a debtor substitutes its foreign currency obligations under a loan agreement for a new payment schedule under a long-term bond, still denominated in foreign currency. This method of substituting one external debt for another could eventually produce a new form of debt conversion, in which banks swap debtors' long-term bonds for domestic equity or local currency.

by private and public sector enterprises. Table 4 shows the yearly quantity of conversions in each category tracked by the central bank, as well as the amount of D.L. 600 foreign direct investment registered since the onset of the debt crisis. Table 5 compares foreign investment levels through the various available mechanisms—principally traditional project finance and debt conversions.

TABLE 4. FOREIGN INVESTMENT AND DEBT CONVERSIONS, 1985-1990

($U.S. millions)

	D.L. 600[a]	Chapter XIX	Chapter XVIII	D.L. 600 loan capital izations	Change of portfolio	Other
			($U.S. millions)			
1985	137	32	115	42	41	89
1986	184	214	411	56	27	276
1987	497	707	696	125	—	451
1988	787	886	909	39	68	1,026
1989	898	1321	410	2	20	104
1990[b]	874	265	293	16	—	46
Total	3,377	3,425	2,834	292	156	2,901
			(percentages)			
Share of total debt conversion	n.a.	36	29	3	2	30

[a]*D.L. 600 total includes all forms of new investment registered under this legislation in the specified year.*

[b]*Figures are through June 30, 1990 except D.L. 600 total, which is through July 11, 1990.*

Sources: Central Bank of Chile internal data; Committee on Foreign Investment internal data; and Robert Behrens and Jorge Kaufmann, "La Estrategia de Desarrollo en Chile y el Papel del Capital Extranjero: 1974-1989," (United Nations Economic Commission for Latin America/ Centre on Transnational Enterprises, May 1991) table 11, p. 93.

TABLE 5. DEBT CONVERSION AND FOREIGN INVESTMENT FLOWS, 1974-1989

($U.S. millions)

	D.L. 600 direct investment[a]	D.L. 600 associated credits	D.L. 600 loan capital-izations[b]	Chapter XIX conversions[c]
1974	-17	19	—	—
1975	-4	54	—	—
1976	-1	36	—	—
1977	16	33	—	—
1978	177	58	—	—
1979	233	72	—	—
1980	170	135	—	—
1981	362	57	—	—
1982	384	0	—	—
1983	132	50	—	—
1984	67	93	—	—
1985	69	57	42	32
1986	19	78	56	214
1987	246	281	125	707
1988	129	632	39	886
1989	169	576	2	1,321
1990	n.a.	n.a.	16	412

[a]*Includes all forms of D.L. 600 investment except loans and loan capitalizations.*

[b]*An additional $11 million in loan capitalizations under D.L. 600 occurred before 1985, but central bank tables do not indicate their precise timing.*

[c]*Includes debt conversions under Annex 2 of Chapter XIX.*

Sources: Behrens and Kaufmann, op. cit., table 10, p. 90; and Central Bank of Chile, Boletín Mensual, No. 755, Jan. 1991, p. 137.

CHAPTER XVIII: DEBT-PESO CONVERSIONS BY CHILEAN RESIDENTS

Chapter XVIII is open to investors without regard to nationality; only Chilean public sector entities and financial institutions are ineligible. In practice, however, only Chilean residents use Chapter XVIII, because foreigners can obtain special tax and financial advantages by channeling conversions through either Chapter XIX or D.L. 600. For Chilean investors, Chapter XVIII offers a different form of incentive: its participants need not reveal the origins of the foreign exchange being converted.[14] Debt conversions are therefore a safe as well as lucrative means of repatriating flight capital.

The liberal regulations governing Chapter XVIII also enable Chilean residents to profit from "round-tripping" their assets. This strategy involves using Chilean funds to purchase dollars on the parallel market[15] and then buying debt on the secondary market and engaging in a debt-peso swap to repurchase local currency at a discount. However, the auction mechanism used to allocate participation in Chapter XVIII limits the profitability and volume of such maneuvers.

The central bank allocates participation in Chapter XVIII on the basis of a biweekly central bank auction. A closed bid identifies the debt that the investor proposes to convert and states what commission the investor is willing to pay the central bank for a conversion right. The central bank establishes the total sum of conversions to be authorized each month in line with its broader monetary policy. The authorities analyze proposed conversions of central bank debt separately from those of other debts, because the government reaps two financial benefits from converting its own foreign obligations into domestic debt: the commission, and a gain from issuing bonds that carry below-market interest rates.

If a Chapter XVIII conversion involves central bank debt, investors who make winning bids at an auction receive bearer bonds from the central bank in exchange for their loan documents. These bonds mature in six years and pay a floating rate below market levels.[16] If, instead, the debt being converted is owed by another debtor, the investor redeems the purchased debt through a local bank, which issues new peso-denominated instruments that pay the investor according to an agreement between it and the debtor.

The result is that an external debt becomes repayable in pesos to a Chilean resident, thereby constituting a "debt-peso" swap. The regulations do not limit investors' use of their local currency proceeds,[17] but neither do they provide access to the formal foreign exchange market if an investor chooses to expatriate the funds. Moreover, investments funded with local currency obtained through Chapter XVIII are not eligible for any tax breaks or other government support that would improve their security or profitability, in contrast with direct foreign investments approved under D.L. 600. Nonetheless, Chapter XVIII has been popular with Chileans because it allows them to join foreigners in reaping profits from the secondary market discount on foreign bank debt.[18]

CHAPTER XIX: DEBT-EQUITY CONVERSIONS BY NONRESIDENTS AND FOREIGNERS

Foreign investors making debt-equity conversions in Chile usually channel funds through Chapter XIX. Central bank regulations governing this mechanism are flexible and open-ended, and many of the norms are unwritten and developed case by case. These rules evolved gradually during the 1985-89 period and were formally revised in April 1990 and again in the spring of 1991. Although the central bank liberalized the rules on capital and dividend repatriation in 1991, most other regulations promulgated before 1990 remain in force alongside the new provisions and therefore remain relevant to understanding the program's record and its current operations.

Eligibility to participate in Chapter XIX extends to foreigners and Chileans residing abroad. Chapter XIX thus goes beyond Chapter XVIII's debt reduction function to serve the additional goal of promoting foreign investment. As part of this investment-promotion effort, Chile enacted Annex 2 of Chapter XIX in September 1987 to enable foreign investors to convert eligible debts into capital in Chilean investment funds.

The central bank considers Chapter XIX conversion proposals individually, rather than using an auction process. Investors submit detailed applications in which, among other things, they must identify the parties to the proposed transaction, the final use of the funds to be converted, and the schedule for disbursement of those funds.

The crucial advantage to converting debt under Chapter XIX, as opposed to Chapter XVIII, is that investors can obtain a right of access to the foreign exchange market to remit future dividends and capital. The central bank does not automatically accord this right as part of Chapter XIX authorizations, but in practice it has granted foreign exchange access to all for-profit Chapter XIX investments.

Although Chapter XIX investors usually receive guarantees of future access to foreign exchange, until 1991 they faced greater initial restrictions on remittances than investors who registered under D.L. 600. Such restrictions exist in most debt-equity conversion programs, propelled by the logic that because the debtor country has prepaid a loan at a profitable rate for the investor, the country should retain the benefit of the investment for roughly as long as it would have held the extinguished loan. In Chile's case, before 1991, investors could not repatriate earnings from Chapter XIX projects during the first four years of an investment, and repatriation was limited during the following four years. In addition, investors could remit capital entering under Chapter XIX only after the tenth year of the investment.

The Aylwin government significantly liberalized the profit and capital remittance rules in 1991, bringing Chapter XIX into line with the D.L. 600 rules. Investors in Chapter XIX projects may now remit dividends immediately and can repatriate their principal three years after their initial investment.[19] The new regulations require investors to compensate the central bank for the discount gained through Chapter XIX if they repatriate funds before the original four- and ten-year deadlines.

The central bank reserves the right to reject Chapter XIX applications without explanation. Despite this rule, officials frequently communicate their concerns about a proposed project to an applicant in an effort to negotiate a more acceptable arrangement and introduce some transparency into the approval process. Although central bank decisionmaking under Chapter XIX is discretionary, participants generally attest to its fairness and objectivity, which suggests that policymakers do convey stable "rules of the game" to investors.

The central bank, under both the Pinochet and the Aylwin governments, has pursued two general lines of inquiry in reviewing Chapter XIX applications. First, officials verify an investor's identity to enforce eligibility policies and reject proposals involving illicit funds. The central bank's second focus in considering Chapter XIX proposals is on the economic qualities of investment projects. Although before 1990 Chile did not promulgate any formal guidelines on project eligibility or policy priorities, de facto preferences and restrictions have existed since the program's inception and have grown more stringent over time. The factors considered by central bank officials fall into four broad categories: 1) the economic sectors in which the investment is proposed; 2) the potential contribution of "new money" for the investment project; 3) the impact of the proposed investment on the country's productive structure—that is, whether the investment would involve a buyout of a private firm, a privatization, a financial restructuring, or the founding of a new enterprise; and 4) the investment's likely effects on Chile's current account balance.

Until April 1990, foreign investments funded through Chapter XIX were subject to the same limits that apply to investments proposed under D.L. 600. The principle of nondiscrimination on the basis of nationality thus governed both D.L. 600 and Chapter XIX investments,[20] with a few exceptions—for example, in the energy sector[21]—that affected both foreign investment programs. Chapter XIX transactions were authorized in a broad range of sectors, ranging from forestry to banking and insurance. However, although foreign investment can still enter the same sectors that the Pinochet regime permitted, concerns about the "denationalization" of Chile's productive structure and the quality of Chapter XIX investments prompted the Aylwin administration to announce important policy changes in 1990. The government formally designated certain types of Chapter XIX investments as priorities and restricted or barred such debt conversions in other sectors.

Priority extends to Chapter XIX investments that establish new enterprises or that will improve the trade balance by expanding existing ones. The 1990 regulations also specify that Chapter XIX funds can continue to flow into nonprofit projects and companies involved in communications and media, energy, tourism, banking, and environmental protection. In a major departure from previous policy, Chapter XIX funds can no longer be invested in financial service enterprises. Acquisitions of capital goods such as airplanes, which can obtain financing from producers or other external sources, are also barred from Chapter XIX, as are most real estate projects.

The central bank created a middle ground for Chapter XIX-financed purchases of existing shares in Chilean companies. Such investments will receive approval only if the investor can show that its funds will provide vital support for a firm's activities or strengthen an existing financial institution. A maximum of 10 percent of the proceeds of a Chapter XIX conversion can be used to purchase existing bank shares, and the central bank will set case-by-case limits for purchases of existing shares in other sectors.

A second issue that the central bank considers in its review of Chapter XIX applications is whether to require that a "new-money" investment accompany the proceeds of a debt-equity conversion. New money, in this context, refers to any equity contribution or foreign currency loan converted at the standard exchange rate, without benefit of a secondary market discount. The issue of new-money requirements stems from concern about "additionality," that is, the fear that debt-equity conversions could reduce the foreign exchange inflows associated with foreign investment by subsidizing projects that would have gone forward anyway and failing to stimulate additional investment.

Until 1990, Chile followed a case-by-case approach to new-money requirements under which the central bank sometimes suggested informally that Chapter XIX applicants fund a portion of their proposed projects through D.L. 600. This approach was most common in the case of large mining projects because the government believed that the presence of a debt conversion discount was unlikely to be the decisive factor in such investment decisions. On the other hand, policymakers rarely pressed for new money in nontraditional export projects, on the theory that such investments were more likely to hinge on the debt conversion incentive. The forestry and paper products industry was an anomalous case, because Chile offers investors a substantial natural advantage in this area, but the central bank nonetheless approved large Chapter XIX investments without insisting on new-money contributions.[22]

The 1990 policy revisions toughened Chile's stance by creating implicit new-money requirements for foreign purchases of existing Chilean assets. For example, because an investor can now purchase only 10 percent of an investment in existing bank shares with Chapter XIX funds, it must marshal other resources for the remainder. A foreign investor facing this limit can invite domestic investors to engage in a joint venture, or it can register funds under D.L. 600 to finance the rest of its desired investment.

As the foregoing description suggests, the central bank considers how a proposed investment under Chapter XIX will affect Chile's productive structure. No formal guidelines existed before 1990 to reflect the relative desirability of Chapter XIX investments that create new enterprises, expand or modernize existing ones, or privatize state-owned companies, as compared to purchases that involve only a change in ownership for an existing private firm. Over time, however, the central bank reportedly reduced the use of Chapter XIX funds for buyouts while continuing to approve equity purchases that would expand an existing company or rescue one from financial distress.

Nonetheless, the authorities approved some controversial buyouts and privatizations under Chapter XIX, prompting criticism that foreign capital enjoyed unfair advantages. In purchasing existing Chilean assets, foreign investors held a substantial advantage over domestic capital both because of the preferential exchange rate offered until recently by Chapter XIX and because they entered the Chilean equity market after a severe recession, when stock prices were notably depressed.[23] The 1990 policy changes formalized the central bank's efforts to re-equilibrate the market for existing equities by limiting the amount of debt conversion financing that foreigners could use for such purchases. In addition, the 1990 regulations specify that foreign investors must prove the necessity of financing working capital or paying off existing financial liabilities before they can obtain authorization to use Chapter XIX funds for such purposes. Export projects are exempt from these restrictions.

Finally, the impact of a proposed investment on Chile's international trade balance influences central bank decisions concerning Chapter XIX. For example, investors whose plans require heavy imports that will not be offset by exports are more likely to encounter pressure to invest at least partially through D.L. 600. Similarly, the central bank reportedly has asked investors to revise Chapter XIX applications that envisioned large royalty payments to a parent or related company in the initial years of an investment, when the pre-1991 regulations prohibited dividend repatriation. The 1990 regulations attempt to protect the national trade balance by specifying that no more than 20 percent of the funds obtained through a debt conversion may cover an investment's import costs.

DEBT CONVERSIONS AND FOREIGN INVESTMENT UNDER DECREE LAW 600

D.L. 600, Chile's general foreign investment law, permits foreign investors to capitalize existing loans to Chilean entities. However, only 3 percent of debt conversions between 1985 and 1989 took this form, perhaps because the central bank preferred to retain maximum policy-making discretion by channeling conversions through Chapter XIX. A review of D.L. 600's provisions nonetheless contributes to an analysis of the Chilean debt conversion program, by describing not only the full range of conversion options but also the rules governing all foreign investments registered under the statute. D.L. 600 offers certain advantages over the Chapter XIX regulations and thus provides useful insights into the role and limitations of the Chilean program.

Only foreigners and Chilean citizens living abroad are eligible to invest or capitalize debts under D.L. 600. Because a debt capitalization by definition involves purchasing equity in a debtor company, debt conversion under D.L. 600 is less flexible than under Chapter XIX, which permits investment in new projects or in existing enterprises that may not have incurred any foreign debts. The Foreign Investment Committee reviews proposed loan capitalizations.[24] In a formally authorized capitalization the investor receives equity in the Chilean firm on terms it has negotiated with the debtor, and this investment is registered in a D.L. 600 contract and is subject to the restrictions and benefits discussed below. Until 1991, one important exception existed. Although D.L. 600 contracts let foreign investors remit earnings at any time and repatriate principal after the third year of an investment, the earnings and capital involved in a D.L. 600 debt capitalization were subject to the more stringent dividend and capital remittance limits contained in Chapter XIX. Now that the Aylwin government has liberalized Chapter XIX's remittance rules, investors who capitalize existing loans can repatriate their funds within the D.L. 600 limits, but they have to compensate the central bank for their debt conversion discount just as Chapter XIX investors must.

The Foreign Investment Committee's review of investment proposals—for both capitalizations and more traditional forms of direct foreign investment—is less thorough than the consideration given to Chapter XIX applications. The secretariat of the committee verifies that an application establishes an investor's nationality, describes the proposed project, provides evidence of any necessary pre-approvals from other agencies, and commits the investor to comply with all relevant national legislation. The committee approves most applications meeting these requirements, although it sometimes asks investors to expand on or reformulate project descriptions to respond to substantive concerns.

Foreign investors receive preferential tax and customs treatment under D.L. 600 and can choose whether to submit to the general corporate tax regime or lock in one of two "tax stability" rates for up to ten years—or twenty years if the investment exceeds $50 million. D.L. 600 also permits investors who have previously elected one of the fixed rates to switch—irrevocably—to the general tax regime. During the implementation stage of a D.L. 600 investment, the investor and project enterprise are also exempt from changes in any indirect taxes and customs duties applicable to the authorized import component of the investment. Now that Chile has returned to democratic rule, tax policies may vary along with the government in power, causing locked-in tax rates to become more valuable to investors.

For export-oriented investment projects of over $50 million, D.L. 600 also lets investors apply for permission to maintain offshore accounts in which they may hold the foreign exchange proceeds of export sales, insurance contracts, and other authorized sources. This privilege makes it easier to secure investment insurance and protects investors from the risks of currency devaluation.

INFORMAL DEBT CONVERSIONS

Almost one-third of the debt conversions recorded by the central bank through June 1990 appear in its catchall "other" category. The largest share of these miscellaneous transactions involves loan prepayments negotiated directly between holders of Chilean debt obligations and their creditors.[25] Because the private financial sector is heavily regulated, the main participants in informal debt repurchases have been private nonfinancial firms and public enterprises. The 1987 and 1988 rescheduling agreements authorized direct repurchases by parastatal borrowers,[26] whereas private prepayments fall outside all formal debt conversion channels.

Direct loan repurchases are financed by borrowers, or purchasers of Chilean debt, either with local currency holdings (which the creditor then converts to foreign exchange on the parallel market) or with foreign exchange held abroad (in which case there is a loan prepayment without any form of conversion). These deals fall within a legal gray area, and some have presumably been financed with funds held abroad in violation of the central bank's foreign exchange controls. The government has not cracked down on this practice; its flexibility may be motivated by a desire to reduce political discontent with the favoritism shown to foreign investors under Chapter XIX. If so, the result is a generous consolation prize, because the government extracts no premium from informal transactions. In addition, the authorities probably favored several high-profile direct debt repurchases, which helped to rescue private firms from dire financial straits,[27] because such transactions promoted national economic recovery.

Informal debt conversions represent the purest case of market forces working to resolve the debt crisis. Because the central bank does not grant access to the official foreign exchange market as part of these deals, no government subsidy exists, and foreign and domestic investors enjoy equal footing.[28] However, the price for such free market purity is that the government receives no commission, and it may have to intervene in the foreign exchange market if private deals put strong upward pressure on the parallel price of dollars. Nonetheless, informal debt repurchases are an intriguing policy alternative to a formal conversion program because they do not discriminate between domestic and foreign capital or create unpredictable future pressures on the formal foreign exchange market.

ACHIEVEMENTS OF THE CHILEAN
DEBT CONVERSION PROGRAM

■ THE POLICY GOALS SERVED BY CHILE'S debt conversion program during 1985-89 are manifest in its regulatory structure and are confirmed in accounts given by the program's architects.[29] Chile pursued an ambitious agenda through debt conversions, with goals ranging from a dramatic reduction in foreign bank debt to privatization of state-owned enterprises and strengthening of existing private firms. In the course of pursuing these goals, the government rejected alternative projects for debt conversion and insisted that several controversial results of the program were worthwhile in light of its overarching objectives.

DEBT REDUCTION

The design and regulation of Chile's multiple debt conversion windows from 1985 to 1989 show that the government's highest priority was to cut the national debt service burden—an urgent task given the sagging domestic investment rate and the huge drain that interest and amortization payments were placing on foreign exchange earnings. Negotiations to reschedule debt payments did not secure the necessary relief, and supplies of fresh loans were dwindling. In 1985, when Chile launched its program, commercial banks were not yet ready to entertain straightforward debt relief as part of the solution to Latin America's macroeconomic troubles. Debt conversions offered them tangible investment opportunities in return for writedowns, and therefore represented a palatable compromise between reschedulings and writedowns. Chile identified conversions as one of its few nonconflictual options for cutting debt service costs and embraced the mechanism wholeheartedly in order to distinguish itself as a cooperative member of the international financial system.[30]

Having decided to employ the incentive of debt conversion, Chilean policymakers took a characteristically relaxed approach to regulating the process. Official priorities or controls rarely affected investor's choices of project form or sector, and the central bank's case-by-case screening process approved a broad variety of lucrative investments.

Furthermore, the government did not explicitly require investors to contribute "new money" at the official exchange rate as a counterpart to Chapter XIX investments. This permissive regulatory structure expedited approval and implementation of debt conversions and supported the program's debt reduction goal. It also contrasted with the more rigid regulations of other debtor nations' conversion programs, thereby providing a powerful advertisement for Chile's hospitable investment climate.

The Chilean government declined to maximize its own financial yield from debt conversions under Chapter XIX by foregoing an auction process (like that used to allocate Chapter XVIII participation) which could have earned it a greater portion of the discount accruing to foreign investors. Policymakers did not want to divert the focus of Chapter XIX from promoting debt conversions to generating public revenues. The central bank did not entirely forego a commission, of course, because it benefited from redenominating its own paper in local currency and from issuing bonds at below-market interest rates in exchange for its foreign debts.

The Chapter XVIII mechanism that allows Chilean residents to participate in debt conversions further illustrates the government's determination to reduce external debt even at the expense of other policy goals. Chapter XVIII gives implicit tax and legal amnesty to holders of flight capital in exchange for their contributions to debt reduction, and it also permits round-tripping of funds held within Chile, thereby allowing Chilean investors to profit from the secondary market discount. As a result, Chapter XVIII buys external debt relief at the expense of potentially inflationary monetary growth and upward pressure on interest and exchange rates.

Although debt reduction was the immediate goal of the program, its long-term objective was to return Chile to the good graces of the international financial system so that voluntary lending could resume. Chile's long exile from the international banking system stemmed from continuing vulnerabilities in its national accounts and from the spillover effects of economic turmoil in other Latin American countries. The 1990 round of rescheduling negotiations between Chile and its creditor banks suggested that this era is nearly over. In the fall of 1990 the banks agreed to reschedule $1.8 billion in principal falling due before 1995, relieving anticipated pressure on foreign exchange supplies over the next few years.[31] In January 1991, Chile secured a small ($320 million) syndicated loan from commercial banks, its first voluntary bank credit since the onset of the debt crisis.[32] Although the sum was low and the interest spread was double that charged on its rescheduled debt, Chile achieved a significant psychological victory by raising new funds in a tight credit market. The country appears to be well on its way to rebuilding a solid credit rating with the international financial community; it reached yet another landmark in this process in the spring of 1991, when commercial banks reportedly removed Chile from their list of "restructuring countries."[33] The causal link between Chile's debt conversion program and its improved relationships with creditor banks remains somewhat speculative, since it is impossible to know what an alternative strategy of tougher bargaining and lower net payments to the commercial banks might have produced. However, the debt conversion program undeniably generated goodwill with commercial banks and reduced the country's stock of bank debt to more manageable levels.

Debt conversion has proved to be an effective and rapid debt reduction tool, and it also furthered other elements of the Chilean structural adjustment program. The side benefits of debt conversion, in the form of investment promotion, funding for private and public sector restructuring, and export promotion, have no doubt made its costs, which include inflationary and exchange rate pressures, distortions in investment incentives, and possible future foreign exchange expenses, more palatable. An understanding of these additional gains helps to illuminate the logic behind Chile's initial regulatory structure.

INVESTMENT PROMOTION

One bonus to promoting debt conversions through Chapter XIX and D.L. 600 was the incentive given to direct foreign investment (DFI). This stimulus complemented Chile's other efforts to attract DFI as a way to generate new foreign exchange flows, improve domestic investment rates, gain access to advanced technologies and management expertise, and encourage export production and market expansion.

The impact of the debt conversion program on DFI levels in Chile cannot be quantified precisely because the answer depends on knowing how much foreign capital would have entered in the absence of this investment incentive. However, ample evidence suggests that conversions have accelerated the pace of foreign investment since 1985. First of all, the program generated a wave of favorable publicity concerning Chile's business climate and economic prospects. For example, in 1983 *Institutional Investor* included Chile on its list of the forty-five least attractive global investment prospects, but in 1989 the country registered the second highest rating in Latin America and the most improved score of any nation.[34] The publicity and goodwill that Chile's debt conversion initiative has engendered are continuing to generate export opportunities as well as investment flows.

One indicator of Chapter XIX's investment promotion effects is the continued rise of D.L. 600 inflows, which surpassed their previous peak in 1987. As a result of the combination of rising Chapter XIX and D.L. 600 investments, Chile now has the second highest level of foreign investment of any Latin American country,[35] albeit at a time when overall investment flows to the region remain depressed. The advent of debt conversions in 1985 did alter the composition of investment registered under D.L. 600 by accelerating a trend in which more loans were registered in proportion to equity investment; this pattern indicates that Chapter XIX conversions displaced some equity purchases. However, this changing mix of financing may stabilize investment-related capital outflows. Furthermore, since 1985 both overall D.L. 600 investment and total equity investment (consisting of Chapter XIX investments and D.L. 600 equity purchases and loan capitalizations) have risen steadily, suggesting that the program has succeeded in generating additional investment in all forms.

Central bank figures on the types of foreign investors who participated in Chapter XIX provide a second means of estimating the program's additionality by facilitating a comparison of the activities of traditional and nontraditional investor groups. Thirty-four percent of authorized Chapter XIX investments from 1985 to 1988 were proposed by commercial banks, few of which would have purchased equity in Chilean enterprises in the absence of such a profitable debt conversion opportunity.[36] On the other hand, the additionality of Chapter XIX investments made by mining enterprises, religious groups, development funds, and multilateral organizations (totaling 14 percent of authorized investments) is dubious because these types of enterprises have ongoing projects in Chile and have been attracted to its economy by longer-term interests. This approach to estimating additionality has serious flaws,

TABLE 6. SECTORAL BREAKDOWN OF FOREIGN DIRECT INVESTMENT AND DEBT CONVERSION, 1982-1990

(percentages)

Sectors	D.L. 600 materializations 1982	D.L. 600 materializations 1985–1990	Chapter XIX authorizations 1985–1990
Mining	24	42	11
Industry	32	21	38
Services[a]	36	33	26
Banking and finance	(n.a.)	(n.a.)	(6)
Insurance	(n.a.)	(n.a.)	(4)
Silviculture	<1	<1	11
Agriculture	3	<1	9
Fishing	5	<1	4

Note: Figures for Chapter XIX reflect authorizations through December 1989; figures for D.L. 600 reflect authorizations through May 1990.

[a]Sectoral information for D.L. 600 and Chapter XIX is broken down in different ways in the official statistics. To compare the data, the following categories were counted as services in the D.L. 600 total: services, transportation, and construction. For Chapter XIX, services were defined as transportation; communications; public utilities; general commerce; social, personal, and community services; and banking and finance.

Sources: Committee on Foreign Investment internal data; Central Bank of Chile internal data.

however. The investments made by commercial banks in such sectors as mining and fishing might have been undertaken by other actors in the absence of Chapter XIX, and traditional investors may have accelerated their activities in response to the debt conversion incentive.

A third approach to estimating additionality is to analyze the sectors that have received debt conversion financing. Table 6 compares a sectoral summary of Chapter XIX activities with the pattern of D.L. 600 investment. These data reveal that a much higher proportion of Chapter XIX investments entered the forestry and agriculture sectors than entered under D.L. 600 before debt conversions began. Chapter XIX thus seems to have stimulated additional activity in these sectors, though nonfinancial factors could also be responsible for the trend. On the other hand, D.L. 600 investment in the industrial and fishing sectors diminished considerably with the appearance of Chapter XIX, suggesting that many projects in these sectors might have gone forward without debt conversions and instead enjoyed a windfall subsidy. The services sector is unique in that its share in D.L. 600 investment has remained fairly stable and it has also attracted a significant portion of Chapter XIX investment. This pattern reflects the investment activities of commercial banks, many of which have converted debts into equity in local banking subsidiaries, pension funds, and other financial service companies.

Table 7 contains a more detailed breakdown of Chapter XIX activities, which indicates that the paper and cellulose industry has received by far the highest proportion of investment. The additionality of this share of foreign investment is questionable, however, given Chile's natural comparative advantage in forestry and wood products and the competitive pressures that are fueling transnational investment in this sector.[37] The additionality of Chapter XIX investment is presumably greater in industries in which Chile has few natural advantages to offer potential investors, such as food products and distribution (7 percent of Chapter XIX investments), chemicals and plastics (3 percent), and restaurants and hotels (3 percent).

A related approach to estimating additionality is to assume that export-oriented investments are most likely to hinge on the debt conversion subsidy, whereas investments in firms that produce for the domestic market are more sensitive to other factors.[38] In light of this test,

Sectors	$U.S. millions	Percentages
Paper	686.1	28
Forestry	256.3	10
Agriculture	183.4	7
Mining	179.8	7
Food production, distribution	165.5	7
Financial Institutions	159.7	6
Fishing	124.8	5
General commerce	91.8	4
Insurance	88.3	4
Chemicals, plastics	82.8	3
Communications	77.3	3
Restaurants, hotels	63.8	3
Other personal or public services	60.0	2
Textiles, leather, shoes	58.1	2
Woods, furniture	56.6	2
Gas, electricity, water	46.8	2
Other	80.5	3
Total of Chapter XIX investment	2,461.6	100

Notes: *Figures reflect investments materialized through June 30, 1989.
Percentages may not total 100 percent because of rounding.*

Source: *Central Bank of Chile.*

Chapter XIX investments in food industries (7 percent), financial services (6 percent), communications (3 percent), and other nontradeables
might well have entered through D.L. 600 in the absence of a debt conversion incentive. Investments in paper (28 percent), forestry (10 percent), agriculture (7 percent), and fishing (5 percent) are much more likely to have involved additionality.

Finally, according to an International Finance Corporation
study,[39] additionality of DFI has probably increased with every year of
the debt program's existence because of the relatively long lead time of

many investment decisions. The authors estimated that 64 percent of Chapter XIX investments were additional, but they also noted that this figure reflects the earliest and most lenient central bank project-screening policies, so that additionality may have increased along with official scrutiny of project proposals. However, the authors disregarded the possible crowding out represented by commercial bank investments in nonfinancial industries and may therefore have presented an overly optimistic portrayal of investment additionality.

STRENGTHENING PRIVATE SECTOR FINANCES

Chile's debt conversion program has complemented government efforts to strengthen the domestic private sector in the wake of damage wrought by the debt crisis. Some form of rescue operation was clearly needed, for a wave of bankruptcies had swept through Chile's industrial sector during 1982-83. The domestic financial sector also suffered a nearly lethal series of blows in 1982, leading to drastically reduced investment rates and delayed economic recovery. Surviving banks had heavy foreign debts, albeit with central bank guarantees, and a significant portion of their earnings had to be earmarked for repurchasing the troubled loans assumed by the government.

Capital infusions from abroad were one means of strengthening Chile's private sector, but investors were predictably unimpressed by the investment climate in Chile from 1982 to 1985. Chapter XIX sparked new interest by effectively subsidizing investors' purchases of local equity. Chapter XVIII, in turn, helped to lower private debt and raise overall private investment levels, although its specific contributions are difficult to document because resident investors need not declare how they use Chapter XVIII funds. More than 60 percent of total debt conversions through mid-1990 involved guaranteed or unguaranteed private sector debts (Table 8), leading to a much faster drop in those loan categories than in direct public sector obligations.

TABLE 8. CHILEAN DEBT CONVERSION BY DEBTOR, 1985-1990

($U.S. millions)

Type of Debtor	Chapter XIX	Chapter XVIII	D.L. 600 capital- izations	Change of portfolio	Other
Public Sector					
Central bank	1,043	545	—	27	906
State bank	284	192	—	5	—
Public enterprises	102	179	—	38	448
Guaranteed private loans	1,973	1,744	2	82	425
(of banks)	(1,973)	(1,744)	(2)	(78)	—
(others)	—	—	—	(4)	(425)
Total	3,402	2,660	2	152	1,779
Private sector					
Financial	22	85	167	—	75
Other	1	89	123	3	1,048
Total	23	174	289	3	1,123
Total	3,426	2,834	292	156	2,901

Notes: Figures reflect materialized investments through June 30, 1990. Figures may not total because of rounding.

Source: Internal data from the External Financial Management Division, Central Bank of Chile.

As suggested by these figures, both the Chilean government and the commercial banks placed top priority on resolving the private sector debt crisis. The government's philosophy of relying on private-sector-led growth complemented the banks' desire to consolidate and strengthen their loan portfolios by eliminating risky private sector exposure. Loan covenants also initially prohibited prepayment or conversion of public sector debts, thus channeling early conversions into private debt.

The fast pace of private debt reduction may still seem surprising because unguaranteed private debts are ineligible for conversion under Chapter XIX, the largest debt conversion channel. However, the government has administered Chapter XIX in a manner that has prevented public debt conversions from creating "disloyal competition" with private debtors. The central bank sets the redenomination rate and bond coupon rate for its own debt conversions low enough to leave room for competitive private sector quotations, and it has not tried to halt the flow of informal debt repurchases that have been especially profitable for private investors. Taken together, these elements of Chilean debt conversion policy have promoted the government's and banks' shared desire to eliminate private sector debts ahead of public sector obligations.[40]

A separate strategy applied to the financial sector's foreign debt because the government had already guaranteed a large portion of it in the course of cleaning up the banking debacle of 1982 and negotiating rescheduling agreements with commercial banks. Some unguaranteed private bank debts were extinguished through D.L. 600 loan capitalizations, in which foreign bank holding companies increased their equity stakes in local subsidiaries in exchange for outstanding loans.[41] Meanwhile, the stock of guaranteed financial sector loans has dwindled considerably as a result of Chapter XVIII and XIX conversions.[42]

The debt conversion program provided an additional boost to local banks' balance sheets by requiring domestic financial intermediation for Chapter XVIII and XIX transactions. According to one estimate, the Chilean banking sector earned fully 25 percent of its income in 1987 from debt conversion fees,[43] although increased competition has greatly reduced such profits in recent years. Some observers note a correspondence between the conversion-related earnings of local banks and the level of their repurchases of loans taken over by the central bank during the financial sector rescue—highlighting an indirect benefit to the government of the debt conversion program.

Last but far from least, debt conversions have contributed to Chile's private sector restructuring by expanding foreign ownership of local assets. Chapter XIX funds have flowed into buyouts of existing Chilean firms, into modernization and expansion projects that give foreign companies a partial stake in ongoing operations, and into the founding of entirely new companies.[44] However, no statistics are available on the proportion of debt conversions financing each of these types of investment, and the categories themselves are of questionable value because they describe only the initial effects of a conversion and do not reflect follow-up investments.[45]

PRIVATIZATION

The Chilean government launched an ambitious privatization program in 1985, announcing initially that twenty-three public enterprises would be partially transferred to private ownership. The privatization effort eventually expanded to involve thirty companies, seventeen of which were scheduled for 100 percent transfer to the private sector.[46] Among the most prominent public enterprises affected were Compañía Telefónica Chilena, the national phone company; Compañía Acero Pacífico, a large steel producer; and several electric utilities.[47] Privatization complemented the Pinochet government's broader goals of reducing the state's size and maximizing private sector activity and the free play of market forces in the economy.

Debt conversions aided the privatization program by providing an additional source of demand for equity in the companies involved. Numerous Chapter XIX conversions were devoted to purchases of newly privatized firms: prominent examples include Chase Manhattan's investments in the international and domestic phone companies; Security Pacific's equity stake in Chile Metro, an electric power utility; and Bankers Trust's investments in Empresa Eléctrica Pilmaiquen, another utility, and in Soquimich, a nitrate company.

Just as important, the debt conversion program reduced the debts of state-owned enterprises, making such companies more attractive to potential private shareholders. The debt buyback clauses in the 1987 and 1988 commercial bank rescheduling agreements opened the door for direct repurchases of parastatal debts and publicly guaranteed private debts, so that firms undergoing privatization could benefit from debt conversions during any stage in their transitions. By June 30, 1990, at least $450 million in foreign debt had been reduced through these clauses.[48]

A final goal of the debt conversion program has been export promotion, which in turn provides Chile with higher foreign exchange income with which to finance debt service and imports. Export earnings have increased dramatically since 1985, but no figures exist to quantify the portion of this improvement produced by conversion-related investment. However, it is safe to say that debt conversions have played a constructive role. According to central bank data, at least 70 percent of Chapter XIX investments through 1989 were in the tradeables sector, although some of these investments represent purchases of existing export capacity. On the other hand, only 11 percent of Chapter XIX transactions funded mining projects, which generated 58 percent of Chile's export earnings in 1988. This suggests that debt conversions are not the leading factor behind the country's successful export record. Their more important contribution has been to support export diversification by increasing investments in nontraditional industries.

. . . .

CRITICISMS OF THE DEBT CONVERSION PROGRAM

■   CHILE'S DEBT CONVERSION PROGRAM has involved many policy trade-offs, and its regulations and very existence remain controversial. Criticisms of the program fall into two broad categories: first, those that argue that the previous government's debt conversion policies were inconsistent with its economic priorities; and second, those that maintain that debt conversion should pursue a different set of goals.[49] Separating these two arguments—which basically differ as to whether the problem with debt conversions is one of means or ends— helps in assessing the nature and impact of the recent policy revisions.

COSTS OF DEBT CONVERSION
WITHIN THE FREE MARKET MODEL

Debt conversions are often described as proof of the "magic of the marketplace": all parties involved benefit from taking advantage of the secondary market for troubled foreign debts.[50] Nonetheless, Chile accepted important trade-offs in deciding to place debt conversions at the center of its debt management policy, and some critics have argued that the Chilean debt conversion regulations involved unacceptable inconsistencies and risks for the Pinochet government's overall economic program.

NONDISCRIMINATION. One controversial point is whether the conversion regulations violate the nondiscrimination principle that has been a hallmark of Chilean foreign investment policy since 1974. Chapter XIX, reserved for nonresident investors, offers several advantages over the rules governing Chilean residents' debt conversion activities under Chapter XVIII. Most important, the auctions that allocate participation in Chapter XVIII tend to reduce the profits accruing to participants as compared with the noncompetitive Chapter XIX application process. Foreign investors can also receive guarantees of future access to the formal foreign exchange market—assurances not available to domestic investors.

On the other hand, foreigners face limits on repatriation of their earnings and capital, whereas resident investors have immediate access to the funds generated by Chapter XVIII conversions and are not restricted in their subsequent use of this local currency. Furthermore, over time the bond coupon rate offered by the central bank for converting its debts under Chapter XIX has dropped well below the market rate, lowering the return on foreigners' conversions until it approximates the profits realized by residents under Chapter XVIII. This phenomenon, and the evident popularity of Chapter XVIII conversions, weaken the argument that Chile's debt conversion program favors foreign investors. In fact, a stronger case can be made that D.L. 600, the basic foreign investment statute, discriminates against Chileans because of its special tax, tariff, and other advantages.

FUTURE FOREIGN EXCHANGE COSTS. A second criticism of debt conversions is that they merely exchange a current debt service obligation for a future—and perhaps more burdensome—foreign exchange cost in the form of dividend and capital outflows. According to this view, the Chilean government should have pursued other avenues of debt reduction, such as negotiated buybacks or securitization deals, to avoid mortgaging future foreign exchange earnings to the uncertain financial plans of transnational companies.

The evidence is not yet in concerning this argument, because the first investments approved under Chapter XIX have not long been eligible to remit dividends. However, a large proportion of Chilean debt conversions—61 percent as of June 1990 (see Table 4)—have not given investors any future access to the official foreign exchange market. Dividend outflows are a concern only for the $3.8 billion in conversions authorized under Chapter XIX and D.L. 600 since 1985. Although uncertainty over the timing and volume of capital outflows related to these investments slightly complicates Chile's macroeconomic planning, the volume of these outflows will be manageable unless a full-blown crisis destabilizes the country's foreign exchange position. Taken as a whole, the Chilean debt conversion effort has successfully limited future foreign exchange commitments and has reduced the prospect of a renewed foreign currency shortage.[51]

EXCHANGE RATE PRESSURES. Chapter XVIII and informal debt conversions create another burden on macroeconomic management by putting upward pressure on the parallel market price for foreign exchange. Participants in Chapter XVIII presumably used some pre-existing foreign currency holdings to purchase debts for conversion, but investors have also used the parallel market to convert Chilean pesos into foreign exchange in order to purchase convertible foreign debts. The central bank indirectly influences parallel market rates by varying the monthly limit on Chapter XVIII transactions and by informally regulating direct debt conversions, to ensure that formal and parallel exchange rates do not diverge dramatically and create pressure for an official devaluation.

The formal and parallel rates have remained relatively close since 1985, suggesting that the central bank has effectively managed the situation. According to official data, the gap between the rates widened in 1988-89 in comparison with the underlying trend, and then narrowed again in 1990. Chapter XVIII transactions peaked at over $900 million in 1988 (Table 6), which contributed to the exchange rate gap by fueling demand for dollars to finance debt conversions. The central bank responded by scaling back the Chapter XVIII quota and then suspending the auction briefly in 1988. However, other factors—notably political uncertainties—probably were more important contributors to exchange rate fluctuations during 1988-89, and reducing the volume of Chapter XVIII transactions gave the central bank a useful policy instrument for offsetting negative trends.[52]

INFLATIONARY PRESSURES. Perhaps the most pervasive criticism of debt conversions is that they are inflationary.[53] The validity of this critique depends on the method that a debt conversion program uses to finance the redenomination of foreign debts in local currency. If a central bank issues local currency to purchase a foreign debt obligation, the resulting increase in the money supply clearly invites inflation. Central bank loans to public or private sector borrowers to finance debt redemptions produce an equivalent effect. However, debt conversions can be structured to neutralize their monetary effects, as Chile has successfully done (see table 2 for inflation figures).[54]

A significant proportion of Chilean conversions has involved informal or formal exchanges in which only existing local or foreign currency reserves have been tapped, thus avoiding inflationary consequences. In contrast, the central bank has had to take active measures to neutralize the inflationary impact of debt conversions involving its own obligations by issuing long-term bonds in exchange for its foreign debts. Both Chapter XVIII and Chapter XIX investors receive long-term government paper in exchange for foreign loan documents, and this financing method delays and distributes the monetary consequences of debt redenominations and also provides the central bank with a flexible policy tool for manipulating the profitability of debt conversions.

Chile's approach to sterilizing the monetary impact of debt conversions requires a well-developed domestic financial market to absorb public long-term bonds. The strength of the Chilean capital market, in turn, stems from several other achievements. First, conservative fiscal practices have kept overall government borrowing at manageable levels, thus leaving ample room for conversion-related bond issues. Furthermore, solid economic growth since 1984 has generated rising demand for financial assets by boosting private savings and pension fund capital, and this in turn has created an impressively wide and deep financial market relative to the national GDP. Foreign investment in the financial sector, including the pension funds, also helped to provide early confidence and new equity infusions to fuel capital market growth. Finally, tax and regulatory policies have promoted financial market development.[55]

Chile's neutralization of the inflationary pressures generated by Chapters XVIII and XIX has entailed costs. The government has competed with the private sector's long-term borrowing needs, thereby crowding out private investment and creating upward pressure on interest rates.[56] Interest payments on the bonds created for debt conversions also constitute a fiscal drain, and these payments may have to rise in the future to keep conversions profitable for investors. Nonetheless, Chile's approach provides an appealing model for non-inflationary debt conversions. However, its success depends on conservative fiscal policies, and on the scope of the domestic financial market, which is determined in turn by both broad macroeconomic factors and specific regulatory measures. Capital market development is a complex endeavor, and for debtor countries whose long-term financial markets are flooded with existing government debt or have yet to be cultivated, foreign debt conversions may threaten to create insurmountable inflationary pressures.

Debt conversion policy thus required trade-offs within the Chilean economic program of 1985-89. Its most serious drawbacks included the differential treatment accorded to foreign and domestic investors, the risks of raising interest rates and crowding out private sector borrowers in the long-term capital market, and the creation of unknown future foreign exchange liabilities. However, these criticisms do not deny the debt conversion program's achievements in terms of its primary goal of debt reduction, nor its benefits for private and public sector restructuring and export promotion. Given these priorities, certain policy revisions might have been appropriate—in particular, instituting a Chapter XIX auction and earmarking a portion of the monetary budget for the local currency costs of debt conversion to reduce the need for government borrowing—but the Pinochet government's use of large-scale debt conversion was basically consistent with its broader economic vision.

ALTERNATIVE PRIORITIES FOR THE DEBT CONVERSION PROGRAM

The priorities underlying Chile's debt conversion program between 1985 and 1989 are also open to challenge. Debt conversion creates an investment subsidy, and many observers argued that this favoritism should be extended only to select investments with particularly desirable qualities.[57] A related concern was that the Chapter XIX screening process did not focus enough on generating additional investment. Finally, many critics condemned the use of Chapter XIX for privatizations and private sector buyouts, arguing that debt conversions subsidized a "fire sale" of Chile's productive structure to foreign interests.[58]

Criticisms challenging the need for this form of investment subsidy acquired greater force as the debt conversion program matured. The overwhelming need in 1985 to cut debt service payments and shore up private companies and banks had largely been met by 1989, with the vital help of debt conversions. In a sense, debt conversions worked themselves out of a job. Only about $5 billion in long-term commercial bank loans remains, out of a total of more than $14 billion outstanding in 1985.[59] The secondary market supply of convertible paper is even smaller than these figures suggest, because many foreign creditors are now satisfied with their portfolios' mix of equity and loans. By 1989, Chilean debt enjoyed the highest secondary market price of any Latin American debtor country, reflecting a shrinking supply, and the price has continued to rise.[60]

Chile has entered a new stage of foreign debt management, in which conversion of commercial bank paper can no longer play a central role. Nonetheless, some potential for debt conversion remains, and the Aylwin government has applied a variety of policy tools to channel such activity.

The central bank announced revised eligibility criteria for Chapter XIX investments in April 1990, in an effort to reduce policymakers' discretion in the project screening process and improve Chapter XIX's efficiency and targeting. The new rules embody a widespread view within the central bank that the program has fulfilled much of its potential and reached a state of "advanced maturity." Debt conversions by foreign investors are now proceeding at a slower pace, reflecting this maturation process.[61]

The central bank's new regulations promote investment quality at the cost of the quantity of future debt reduction. The restrictions imposed on Chapter XIX have channeled a greater proportion of the remaining deals into Chapter XVIII; in the first four months of 1991, nearly ten times more debt was converted under Chapter XVIII than under Chapter XIX.[62] However, the rising secondary market price of Chilean debt, economic uncertainties connected with the Persian Gulf War, and a global economic downturn are intervening variables that make it difficult to trace the precise impact of the policy revisions.

The new targeting of investment subsidies under Chapter XIX may also improve the additionality of debt-conversion-financed investment projects. Investment decisions in the export and import-competing sectors are most likely to be influenced by a subsidy to their startup costs, because such projects will be exposed to global competition. Chile's decision to encourage such investments and eliminate Chapter XIX participation in nontradeables sectors such as finance and construction should thus help to increase the additionality of the debt conversion program. On the other hand, as the marginal returns on Chapter XIX transactions are reduced by market forces, additionality may decline.

Finally, the 1990 regulatory revisions will reduce pressures on the long-term bond market by lowering the total level of conversions that the central bank must sterilize. This benefit will be offset, however, by the heavily public sector profile of Chile's remaining foreign debt, because conversions of such debt require sterilization, whereas direct private and public sector enterprise deals do not. Chile could address this problem by linking further conversions of public sector debt to privatizations, as Argentina has done. A golden opportunity for the implementation of this strategy will arise if analysts are correct in predicting that Codelco, the giant state-owned copper company, will be privatized.[63]

The Aylwin government risked eroding investor confidence in the country's business climate by altering the debt conversion norms soon after assuming power. Restricting the eligibility of foreign investments for Chapter XIX could have signaled to the international financial community that the new government was willing to tinker with other aspects of the country's investment climate, or that it did not adequately value policy stability. The investment-promotion value of Chile's debt conversion program has been one of its most important contributions to economic recovery, and this reputational interest merits careful maintenance. However, Chilean officials stress that many of the new guidelines, including the limits on imports and working capital expenditures, merely enunciate preexisting policies—the fundamental "rules of the game" have not been affected. Furthermore, the natural erosion of the profitability of debt conversions means that the new sectoral limits do not impose high costs on investors who must now go through D.L. 600. And because remaining commercial bank creditors are largely satisfied with their existing portfolios of Chilean equity and loans, the revised Chapter XIX regulations do not greatly affect the interests of this important audience. The international financial community seems to have recovered from jitters about Chile's transition to democracy, and changes in the priorities emphasized by the debt conversion program have not played a major role in assessments of the country's future prospects.[64]

LESSONS FROM THE
CHILEAN EXPERIENCE

■   THE CHILEAN DEBT CONVERSION PROGRAM provides valuable information for other debtor countries on the potential achievements, limitations, and life span of such an effort. Its results should be judged by the goals that Chile has assigned to it, but its benefits and failings also highlight alternative policies that would better serve other goals.

In a liberal domestic and foreign investment climate such as Chile's, debt conversions have proved valuable for stimulating external debt reduction. The government's top priority, and its most clear-cut achievement, has been to lower the country's outstanding commercial bank debt and thereby return to voluntary participation in the international financial market. Official and commercial bank preferences coincided to produce especially rapid debt reduction in the private sector, and conversions also accelerated the privatization of state-owned companies. One result of Chile's cooperative and expedited approach to debt conversion has been the promotion of the country's overall investment climate: the conversion program should be credited with improving private investment levels generally as well as with directly stimulating investment through the creation of a foreign exchange subsidy.

Chile deliberately minimized its efforts to target the investment generated by debt conversions because it placed a higher priority on debt reduction. The central bank approved large Chapter XIX investments in the paper and forestry sectors, where Chile enjoys a strong natural advantage, and a smaller number of debt conversions were devoted to the mining sector despite the questionable additionality of such subsidized investments. Many Chapter XIX transactions served the government's goals of strengthening ailing private companies and boosting exports, but the overriding emphasis on debt reduction led to some deals that cannot be justified in terms of these priorities.

Another policy trade-off implicit in the Chilean debt conversion program concerns participation by domestic investors. Chapter XVIII conversions and direct debt repurchases produced more than half of all debt reduction up to mid-1990. In choosing to rely so heavily on its own private sector to arrange and finance debt reduction, Chile has success-fully reduced the future foreign exchange cost of its debt conversion pro-gram. It has also lowered the need for public sector financing of the for-eign debt by tapping private sector savings. On the other hand, the cen-tral bank has had to turn a blind eye to instances of tax evasion and the bending of foreign exchange rules, because private sector participation in foreign debt conversions often involves such irregularities. Domestic purchases of foreign debt for conversions have also placed pressure on the informal exchange rate, which may have interfered with official exchange rate targets, but which at the same time provided a useful tool for influencing the parallel rate.

The great vice of debt conversion for many debtor countries has been its fueling of excessive monetary growth. Chile has largely avoided this problem by selling long-term bonds through its domestic capital market in order to sterilize debt redenomination expenditures. A pre-requisite to controlling the inflationary effects of debt conversion is thus the cultivation of a deep and broad long-term capital market, which in turn requires fiscal discipline, a growing supply of domestic savings, healthy financial institutions, and regulations that permit active financial intermediation. And even with a strong capital market, Chile's debt con-version program has entailed costs by sapping demand for long-term instruments and putting upward pressure on interest rates.

The Aylwin government weighed these trade-offs and decided to prohibit direct buyouts and improve the overall quality of investment obtained through debt conversions, at the cost of slowing the rate of debt reduction. This policy implies the continued acceptance of some dis-tortions, because any debt conversion involves a preferential exchange rate, but one bias in the system is being tackled: the interest rates cur-rently offered on the central bank's debt conversion bonds nearly equal-ize the profits available to domestic and foreign investors engaging in formal conversions. However, Chile's program is now bumping up against another iron rule of debt conversions: its capital market is virtu-ally saturated with long-term bonds, and the central bank may have to hike coupon rates if it wants to promote further debt swaps.

A final lesson from Chile's experience is that debt conversions have a limited life cycle and are most apt for various purposes during differing stages of this cycle. Allowing an early rush of deals offers the best prospect for quick debt reduction, but not for investment additionality. When market forces begin to cut into conversion profitability, debt reduction may continue apace, but governments should no longer count on generating much revenue—for themselves or for financial intermediaries—through debt conversions. If maintaining cooperative relations with creditors and investors is a high priority, a government may be wise to wait until conversions have slowed of their own accord before introducing potentially controversial regulatory changes, as Chile has done.

On the other hand, debtor countries can prolong or quicken the life cycle of debt conversion through their initial choice of policies. If Chile had more narrowly restricted Chapter XIX participation from the beginning, there would be more room for profitable conversions today because a larger stock of debt would remain on the books at a lower price. However, had Chile taken this approach, it might not now be attracting voluntary credits from the private capital markets. This achievement indicates the value of the country's previous conversion efforts without establishing whether a more selective approach to debt conversion might have performed as well or better. The conversion regulations of 1990 take a more sedate, circumspect approach to debt-equity conversion, and at least in the unfolding new era this appears to be the most useful path.

Part III
Debt Conversion
in Other Major
Debtor Countries

DEBT CONVERSION IN
OTHER MAJOR DEBTOR COUNTRIES

■   NO OTHER COUNTRY IN LATIN AMERICA has followed Chile in placing debt conversions at the center of its debt management strategy. Nonetheless, most countries have experimented with various debt conversion programs—at times under pressure from their bank creditors—and the pace of programs in Argentina and Mexico has recently increased. A brief review of the history and current status of debt conversion policies in these countries and in Brazil shows that debt conversions are not likely to reprise the starring role they have assumed in Chile. Debt conversions, however, may contribute importantly to continuing structural adjustment programs by spurring investment in certain economic sectors and complementing privatization efforts. In fact, as the following case studies suggest, debt conversion programs in the "big three" debtor countries may generate many of the side benefits and costs that Chile experienced, while leaving to other policies much of the task of debt reduction.

ARGENTINA'S EXPERIENCE

■   ARGENTINA HAS ENDURED A DECADE of economic stagnation and crisis management, and the history of its debt conversion program reflects this unstable policy climate. Informal debt conversions occurred in Argentina as early as 1984, and the government launched a formal program in 1987 to induce commercial banks to agree to a debt restructuring package that included exit bonds.[65] However, inflationary concerns forced it to suspend that program in April 1990. Most recently, Argentina has launched an ambitious privatization scheme that relies on high volumes of converted debt to purchase such assets as Aerolineas Argentinas and the national phone company, ENTEL.

Debt conversion policy has only recently become a leading component of Argentina's debt management efforts, which previously centered on reschedules, new money accords, and extended buildups of interest arrears (currently totaling $7 billion). Even now, the country's foremost goal is to negotiate a Brady Plan debt reduction agreement, and the flurry of recent debt swaps and privatizations should be viewed in the context of that goal, which if realized could erase as much as 35 per cent of Argentina's bank debt.[66] Debt conversions and the associated privatizations are helping to restore banks' confidence in Argentine economic management. They are also valuable promoters of domestic and foreign investment. In particular, the profitability of converting Argentine debt—which sold at discounts of more than 85 percent until recently—has encouraged investments by both foreign and domestic entities that would otherwise have shied away from the Argentine economic morass.

Argentina operated a formal debt conversion program from 1987 to 1990, with intermittent revisions and suspensions. Roughly two-thirds of debt conversions undertaken during this period were devoted to purchases of Argentine equity by both domestic and foreign investors, which assisted the government's uphill struggle against domestic capital flight and the heavy net capital outflow associated with the foreign debt. The remaining one-third of debt reduction arranged under the 1987 program stemmed from an on-lending scheme and a mechanism whereby various private sector obligations to the central bank could be extinguished in exchange for contributions of foreign exchange. Argentina used the latter two programs to channel resources into the capital-starved private sector without the intermediate step of a government guarantee program for private business debts such as the one employed in Chile.

Investment proposals generally qualified for the original Argentine debt conversion program if they involved imports of new capital goods or promised to improve the country's balance of payments. In addition, the government initially required investors to fund half of their proposed investments with money that did not benefit from the debt conversion subsidy. However, the authorities soon relaxed this rule to 30 percent in response to pressures from bank creditors, who were finding it difficult to unload their Argentine loans on the secondary market.

Argentina tinkered with a second policy variable by switching from use of the official foreign exchange rate to the parallel market figure early in the course of its formal debt conversion program.

Argentina possesses neither a well-developed long-term capital market nor a stable inflationary picture, and so the government could not issue large quantities of long-term domestic bonds to defray the inflationary effect of the capital inflows attracted by debt conversions. Instead, the country limited the debt reduction ambitions of its conversion program. From 1988 until its suspension, the program operated with an annual conversion ceiling of $300-400 million, which allowed Argentine authorities to be relatively selective about the investment projects they allowed to benefit from conversions.

However, policymakers emphasized revenues over investment selectivity, endeavoring to capture the largest possible share of the secondary market discount on Argentine debt. The program used an auction to allocate conversion rights among previously approved projects, maximizing the government's financial benefit and placing foreign and domestic investors on equal footing in their efforts to profit from the secondary market. Because the discount on Argentine debt reached 75 percent by 1989, the government had ample room to repay its foreign debts at a fraction of their face value while still offering investors an incentive to import capital into the country. The annual ceiling on debt conversions gave the authorities further leverage in extracting a high share of the discount for the national coffers, because this limit fostered competition for conversion rights.

Thus, although the formal conversion program had little impact on Argentina's burgeoning foreign debt, it enabled the country to repay some foreign loans at a heavy discount and attract additional private investment. Data on the types of investment generated by the 1987-1990 program[67] suggest that Argentina's selective conferral of auction participation rights may have succeeded in improving the quality and quantity of incoming foreign investments. Central bank figures for 1988 show that tourism received the largest share of conversion-related financing. Such projects are solid foreign exchange earners, and although the extent of additionality of investments in tourism is hard to know, some investors were no doubt encouraged to take a gamble because of the debt conversion subsidy. Furthermore, the debt conversion program attracted a high level of investment in Argentina's automotive sector, in which the country offers neither a comparative advantage nor (because of ongoing structural reforms) a heavily protected market. The debt conversion incentive may have been decisive in attracting such investments.

The Argentine program incurred the same costs as those identified in the Chilean case, but in the context of chronic macroeconomic instability those costs eventually became unbearable. Purchases of foreign debts for conversion exacerbated pressures on the parallel rate for Argentine currency, destabilizing the government's attempts to manage exchange rates. Financing the conversions also had inflationary repercussions.[68] Debt conversions were not the biggest culprit in Argentina's macroeconomic difficulties—fiscal imbalances were the primary problem—but managing the program's costs within a chaotic economic context proved impossible, and the government eventually closed the conversion window to concentrate on fundamental stabilization and adjustment measures.

Since 1990, Argentina's debt conversion program has functioned on an ad hoc basis, but it is now more central to the country's macroeconomic and debt management strategies than in its previous incarnation. Argentina has adopted the promising tactic of linking debt conversions to privatizations. The government of Carlos Menem is administering an ambitious privatization program and after some delays has closed several significant privatization deals. For example, domestic and foreign investors are purchasing 60 percent of equity in ENTEL and have agreed to convert more than $5 billion in foreign debt as part of the arrangement.[69] This amounts to a payment of roughly $1 billion for Argentine debt on the secondary market, compared with additional cash outlays of only $214 million. Debt conversions played a substantial role in the privatization of Aerolineas Argentinas as well, with $2 billion in Argentine debt, similarly purchased for approximately 20 cents on the dollar, being added to $260 million in cash as the price of an 85 percent stake in the airline.

These and other privatization-related debt conversions may extinguish a sizable portion of Argentina's $33 billion stock of foreign commercial bank debt. The strategy of permitting large debt conversions to finance major privatizations on a case-by-case basis lets Argentina sweeten the pot for important potential investors while maintaining leverage over the outcome. The Argentine plan also avoids the specter of inflation because the government is repurchasing the debts with existing state assets rather than newly printed money. Furthermore, to the extent that Argentina is selling off money-losing assets that contributed to its chronic budgetary problems, the combined privatization and debt conversion program will help to stabilize the country's fiscal outlook and dampen inflation.

This ad hoc approach to debt conversions has drawbacks, however. One is the loss of an opportunity to establish transparent and stable policies that could attract a broader range of investors. The example of Chile suggests that a long-term and diversified debt conversion program can serve as an excellent public relations tool that lures investors to sample the achievements of an economic reform program. In addition, investors are finding it difficult to purchase the huge quantities of debt necessary to complete recent privatization deals, and arguments have erupted over whether the rising price of Argentine debt should be factored into a revised purchase price.[70] Argentina might benefit from drafting new regulations that formalize and expand its current debt conversion norms so that more modest but cumulatively valuable transactions can go forward.

The linking of debt conversions with privatization also invites criticism that Argentina has sold off its national patrimony for a paltry sum. One prong of this criticism is fundamentally a condemnation of privatization programs, at least in a recessionary environment such as Argentina's, but the privatization debate is beyond the reach of this essay. The second controversial aspect of Argentina's current program is its use of productive assets to repurchase foreign debts that might instead be rescheduled or extinguished through negotiations or a moratorium on debt service.

Argentina probably could not negotiate a Brady Plan agreement, however, without offering substantial progress on privatizations, and the debt conversion program has in turn made privatization a viable policy. Thus the Argentine debt conversion program is integral to the country's overall approach to unwinding the debt crisis. Short of rupturing relations with the international financial system by declaring a formal debt service moratorium—an approach tried but abandoned by both Brazil and Peru—Argentina's only option is to pursue some form of rapprochement with creditors, for which debt conversion is proving very helpful. The program thus serves both national and creditor interests while minimizing undesirable side effects. With some revision and the addition of large-scale debt reduction through a Brady Plan agreement, the newest Argentine debt conversion program could help put the country onto a sustainable growth path.

. . . .

DEBT CONVERSION SCHEMES IN BRAZIL

■ BRAZIL'S ECONOMIC CRISIS WAS RELATIVELY LATE blooming, but it has proved tenacious. The country has embarked on numerous stabilization plans but has yet to display signs of a long-term economic recovery. In the meantime, Brazil has had a tumultuous relationship with its commercial bank creditors, and no resolution is yet in sight for the country's enormous debt management problems. Brazil imposed a moratorium on debt service in February 1987, and although this policy formally ended in 1988, Brazil has again fallen behind in its payments and owed $9 billion in arrears by the spring of 1991.[71] A recently negotiated restructuring agreement covering those arrears is providing modest new hope for Brazil, and attention is turning to other elements of the country's economic policy, including the potential for debt conversion.

Debt conversions have occurred in Brazil since at least 1982, but no formal program has survived long in the country's unstable policy environment. The multiplicity and informality of Brazilian debt conversion mechanisms makes it difficult to compare its norms to those of other Latin American debtor nations. Nonetheless, Brazil's experience with formal conversion programs illustrates many of the same dilemmas that other countries have confronted, and it therefore offers a useful focal point for analyzing Brazilian debt swaps.

Foreign investment has traditionally played an important role in the Brazilian economy, and declines in these foreign capital inflows prompted the Brazilian authorities to launch their first debt conversion plan. This program, which began in 1982, employed tax incentives to encourage the capitalization of relending operations for foreign enterprises.[72] In 1984 Brazil revised this policy by authorizing direct loan capitalizations, which were carried out without any discount to face value. Although this initiative provided no tax incentive, it garnered an impressive $2 billion in investment.

The 1987 moratorium on debt service payments prompted a rapid decline in the secondary market price of Brazilian debt and opened up more lucrative opportunities for would-be participants in debt conversions. As a result, domestic and foreign investors joined commercial banks in pushing the government to broaden the scope of its debt conversion program,[73] and in response new rules appeared in November 1987. One new mechanism permitted the conversion on a case-by-case basis of nonmature debts and resulted in swaps involving roughly $850 million in foreign bank debt. In the second conversion window, investors bid in monthly central bank auctions that allocated conversion rights totaling $150 million on the basis of the proportion of the discount investors offered to the central bank. Participants in these auctions had to calculate their bids on the basis of the official exchange rate, thus creating an additional cost for them. The auctions were substantially oversubscribed,[74] and one report estimates that the Brazilian government retained 50 percent of the secondary market discount on debts converted through the auction system.[75]

In addition to attempting to maximize its share of the secondary market discount via an auction system, Brazil's formal debt conversion program used several broad guidelines to channel the investments that benefited from its debt conversion program toward priority projects. Proposed investments qualified for the debt conversion program under the same relatively liberal regulations applied to all foreign investment, with the exception that regulators barred purchases of shares in existing companies if the proposed investments appeared to denationalize Brazilian industries. In addition, the government reserved 50 percent of each monthly quota for investments in four lesser-developed Brazilian states.

The conversions registered under this formal mechanism were dwarfed by the flow of informal conversions during 1987-88,[76] so the program's investment and capital remittance guidelines did not affect the majority of investments made through debt conversion. Although Brazil sought to gain financial benefits and desirable investments from its debt conversion program, in reality the most significant contribution of the conversions, because of their heavily informal nature, was to reduce the stock of foreign debt. By one estimate, at least 10 percent of Brazil's debt to foreign commercial banks was converted during 1988 alone.[77]

Much of the debt conversion boom involved financial arbitrage, in which investors profited from purchasing and exchanging foreign debts but did not invest the local currency proceeds in productive assets within Brazil. The high volume of debt conversions in 1988 thus provided few long-term benefits to Brazil beyond its debt reduction impact. At the same time, it generated high costs. Purchases of foreign debts for conversion, and demand for foreign exchange to safeguard conversion-related profits, strained Brazil's foreign exchange reserves to the limit. In addition, the monetary effects of the debt conversion program contributed to hyperinflationary pressures. These concerns, and persistent political criticism of the subsidies involved, led the government to cancel its formal program in January 1989.

The history of debt conversions in Brazil parallels the country's difficulties in many areas of economic management, where political pressures and destabilizing economic forces have caused the failure of a long series of reform programs. Investor confidence has been dismal, and in such an atmosphere neither a formal nor a free-market-based approach to debt conversions is likely to achieve the desired results. The boom in Brazilian debt conversions during 1988 produced all the worst side effects of such transactions, including declining foreign exchange supplies, rising inflation, and soaring black-market prices for dollars. However, the fundamental cause of these maladies was Brazil's chaotic economic climate rather than its experiment with a formal debt conversion mechanism.

Brazil's new round of rescheduling talks with its commercial bank creditors may produce fresh accords on debt conversions. The banks will reportedly seek the right to convert up to one third of any new loans into equity at 100 cents on the dollar.[78] Meanwhile, the Brazilian central bank issued regulations in May 1991 to allow debt-equity conversions that are linked to privatizations, as long as they occur at no less than a 25 percent discount,[79] and it has also promulgated rules for debt-for-nature swaps. Even if the parties agree on a middle ground between these frameworks for debt conversion, significant privatizations are not yet occurring, and macroeconomic instability persists. As a result, the future role of debt conversions in Brazil remains uncertain.

······································

MEXICO'S DEBT REDUCTION CAMPAIGN

■ MEXICO HAS BEEN LATIN AMERICA'S leader in the debt crisis, however unappealing this title may be. The near-default by Mexico on its foreign bank loans in August 1982 precipitated the crisis, and Mexico was also the first country to obtain a new-money and rescheduling package from commercial banks. Later, Mexico pioneered debt securitizations as part of a new "menu" approach to addressing the needs of both creditors and debtors. Most recently, Mexico became the test case for the Brady Plan, which is currently the most prominent international strategy for alleviating Latin America's debt burden.

Such leadership does not extend to the debt conversion arena, however. Mexico has emphasized negotiated debt restructurings as a means of tackling its foreign debt burden, and its foreign investment policies have centered on taking advantage of the country's proximity to U.S. markets. More recently, as part of its efforts to solidify far-reaching economic reforms, Mexico has launched a privatization program that provides another important mechanism for attracting foreign capital. Debt conversions have not played a central role in any of these international economic policies. Nonetheless, Mexico's 1985 and 1987 rescheduling agreements with commercial banks created a legal framework for debt conversions, and two stages of conversions have ensued.[80]

Mexico's first debt conversion program, which began in 1986, was designed to complement the country's early structural adjustment efforts. The program endeavored to attract investment in priority activities—defined to include privatizations, export-oriented investments, and projects that incorporated new technology or increased the level of national content in the goods produced. Mexico used the innovative but bureaucratically cumbersome approach of varying the processing fees it charged investors according to the priority it attached to a given debt conversion proposal. No fees applied to proposals in the highest priority categories, and the maximum possible fee was 25 percent of the face value of the debt proposed for conversion. Foreign investors also had to reckon with Mexico's restrictive 1973 Law to Promote Mexican Investment and Regulate Foreign Investment, which restricted foreign investment levels and destinations, although liberalization of these rules occurred in the late 1980s. The main window of the debt conversion program was open only to foreigners, and Mexican investors operated through a smaller pilot program.[81]

Mexico converted a total of $3.2 billion in commercial bank debt through this program.[82] This figure incorporates conversion-financed investments approved through 1988, although Mexico did not accept any new conversion proposals after November 1987 except those tied to privatizations. The inflationary effects of debt conversions prompted the shutdown, which mirrored decisions later taken in Brazil and Argentina. Mexico thus provides another example of a large economy unable to undertake substantial debt conversions because its capital market could not absorb long-term instruments that would offset the liquidity generated by trading foreign debt for domestic funds.

Mexico's government also retrospectively condemned the conversion program for failing to generate additional foreign investment and for discriminating against domestic investors. The program's authors had evidently accepted these flaws and concentrated on designing a program that limited the debt conversion subsidy to high-priority sectors including *maquiladoras,* the automotive industry, and tourist projects.[83] Mexico maintained leverage over investment quality by opting not to use an auction to allocate conversion rights. However, the regulations thus allowed government officials to exercise a high degree of discretion in apportioning subsidies to proposed foreign investments, and this constituted a form of interference with market forces that contradicted Mexico's general shift toward economic liberalization. Shutting down the conversion program thus served the goals of both policy consistency and macroeconomic management.

In the meantime, Mexico exerted other forms of leverage to wrest concessions from its foreign creditors. As a result of arduous and repeated negotiations with creditor banks, Mexico has managed to reverse the growth of its overall foreign debt.[84] This accomplishment did not require providing windfall gains to private investors through a liberal debt conversion program such as Chile's. Mexico scored this success not only because of its tough bargaining position, but because creditors and their governments were persuaded that Mexico's nascent economic transformation merited encouragement in the form of debt reduction. Moreover, Mexico's recent record in gaining concessions from its creditors based on its good behavior was greatly facilitated by the country's large size and proximity to the United States.

Mexico has recently embarked on a new approach to debt conversion that makes further debt reduction its foremost goal. The program has succeeded in attracting strong investor interest: Mexico established a $3.5 billion limit for debt conversions in 1990-93, and by October 1990 conversion rights for this entire sum had been auctioned off.[85] If Mexico succeeds in liberalizing and strengthening its domestic financial system,[86] enabling it to offset the inflationary impact of debt conversions, a new quota of conversions could be announced before 1993. However, the government reportedly believes that it can attract private investment without the conversion incentive, and that it will not need further debt relief.[87] A middle course would be to allow future debt conversions only in the context of privatizations, as Argentina has done, to maximize both the financial and structural adjustment benefits of the conversion tool. However, if Mexico's policymakers are correct in anticipating that adequate unsubsidized private capital will materialize to carry out planned privatizations, including that of the nationalized banking system, the country will do best to proceed without a debt conversion program.

Part IV
Comparisons
and Conclusions

COMPARISONS AND CONCLUSIONS

■   A CLOSE LOOK AT DEBT CONVERSIONS in Latin America shows that they are neither the cure nor the curse that some observers have claimed. Not surprisingly, the success of debt conversion policies in achieving the goals a government has selected for them—and in minimizing negative side effects—depends on the overall coherence and stability of a national economic program. In Brazil, debt conversions have produced destabilizing short-term capital flows far more often than additional long-term investments, but this does not reflect an official policy. Instead, Brazil's failure to stabilize its national economy extends to impotence in stemming informal conversions. At the opposite end of the spectrum, two successive Chilean governments have overseen debt conversion programs, involving both formal and informal transactions, that required only minor exertions to counteract their negative side effects, because the economy has been stable and could be fine-tuned with available policy instruments.

Beyond the pressing need for coherent economic policies to back debt conversion programs, several more specific lessons emerge from the four case studies presented here.

1) For countries that do not possess a well-developed long-term capital market, the inflationary effects of debt conversions can be minimized by tying them to privatization efforts and setting a ceiling on the volume of conversions (the Argentine and Mexican cases).

2) Debt conversions can assist in private sector recovery and restructuring by attracting additional capital from both foreign and private investors, generating fees for domestic financial intermediaries, and improving confidence in a country's investment outlook (the Chilean and perhaps the Argentine case).

3) Rapid debt reduction is not necessarily a rational goal for debt conversions, especially where high inflation exists. Such debt reduction may occur at the expense of a run on foreign exchange that later makes it impossible to service foreign debts, leading to a buildup of arrears that in turn replenishes the stock of foreign debt (the Brazilian case).

4) As a country improves its investment climate, it will lessen the financial advantages of engaging in debt conversions, because the secondary market price of its debts will rise in response to growing demand. The faster a debt conversion program reduces a country's outstanding obligations, the shorter its life cycle will be and the fewer opportunities it will have to channel investment in desired directions (compare the Mexican and Chilean cases).

5) A government may enhance the additionality of debt conversion-financed investments by encouraging the participation of nontraditional investors and placing top priority on tradeable and nontraditional sectors. Conversely, permitting debt conversions to finance buyouts of existing enterprises or to invest in sectors with a strong natural advantage will undermine additionality (the Chilean case).

6) Although channeling investment conversions into preferred sectors may improve additionality, applying a priority system risks creating favoritism and corruption. Even if projects are screened objectively, government intervention in the conversion process may contradict ongoing efforts to improve the responsiveness of private investment to market signals (policymakers have wrestled with this dilemma in the Argentine, Chilean, and Mexican cases).

7) Debt conversion norms that permit domestic investors to participate on roughly equal terms with foreign capital will reduce the distorting effects of conversions, and will minimize foreign exchange costs by avoiding the need to guarantee future access to formal foreign exchange markets (the Chilean case).

8) To minimize a country's debt redemption costs and the level of investment subsidy created by debt conversions, a program should be structured to require investors to compete for participation rights. However, other priorities—notably improving relations with creditors and private investors—weigh against employing such a structure (experiments with both approaches are found in the Mexican and Chilean cases).

9) Debt conversion programs often serve as bargaining chips in debt negotiations and can help to win concessions from creditors. However, in some circumstances debt reduction can be negotiated without a debt conversion incentive (compare the Argentine and Mexican cases).

10) Despite the burgeoning list of countries engaging in privatizations and other structural adjustments, debt conversion mechanisms embedded in a solid economic program can still generate substantial investor interest, allowing the debtor country to redeem its debts at a relatively low cost (the Argentine and Mexican cases).

These conclusions do not prescribe the outlines of a single optimal debt conversion policy. Such a model policy depends on country-specific factors including the macroeconomic environment, capital market development, and political forces. Debtor countries' bargaining strategies for managing their external debt also vary considerably and may play a large role in determining their handling of debt conversions. If a country decides to hold out for high volumes of negotiated debt relief, it may choose to delay debt conversions in order to use them as a bargaining chip, or it may employ debt conversions to serve other goals such as investment promotion.

Implementation of a debt conversion program is most important for a country that needs to win the goodwill of investors and creditors. Undeniably, debt conversions entail buying friends: a debtor country offers the prospect of profitable deals in order to reengage itself in the international financial system. Just as clearly, debt conversions by themselves are not a magic wand that can mend fractured relationships between a government and its potential suppliers of private capital. Countries should avoid a boom and bust pattern in debt conversion policies by implementing programs only after stabilization programs have begun to take hold, limiting their programs to sustainable volumes of conversions, and closely monitoring informal conversion channels.

Debt conversions have largely worked themselves out of a job in Chile, and they could be a short-lived vehicle for debt management in other countries if ongoing structural adjustment programs and alternative debt reduction plans take hold. The secondary market price of debts from all four of the countries studied here has been rising, with Chilean and Mexican debt registering especially substantial gains. Economic recovery will improve domestic and foreign investment levels, making debt conversion subsidies to investment less justifiable. At the same time, as foreign debts become more expensive, the subsidy offered by debt conversion mechanisms dwindles. If Latin America returns to healthy growth rates in the 1990s, debt conversion programs may be neither a pandemic nor a panacea, but simply irrelevant.

Notes

1 One article that recently reached this conclusion is Stephen Fidler, "Going Out of Style: Debt-Equity Conversion," *The Financial Times*, April 5, 1991, p. 31.

2 For more extensive analysis of the Pinochet government's economic policies, see Alejandro Foxley, *Latin American Experiments in Neoconservative Economics* (Berkeley: University of California Press, 1983); Sebastian Edwards and Alejandra Edwards, *Monetarism and Liberalization: The Chilean Experiment* (Cambridge, MA: Ballinger, 1987); Laurence Whitehead, "The Adjustment Process in Chile: A Comparative Perspective," in Rosemary Thorp and Laurence Whitehead, *Latin American Debt and the Adjustment Process* (Pittsburgh: University of Pittsburgh Press, 1987), pg. 117-161; and Barbara Stallings, "The Political Economy of Democratic Transition: Chile in the 1980s," in Barbara Stallings and Robert Kaufman, eds., *Debt and Democracy in Latin America* (Boulder: Westview Press, 1989), pp. 181-199.

3 These figures reflect the nominal value of the debt, as reported by the central bank.

4 An excellent overview of Chile's economic program during the "neoliberal" period is Joseph Ramos, "Políticas de estabilización y ajuste en el Cono Sur, 1974-1983," *CEPAL Review*, No. 25, April 1985, pp. 85-109. The links between Chile's financial liberalization and its external debt crisis are explored in Ricardo Ffrench-Davis, "El Problema de la Deuda Externa y la Apertura Financiera en Chile," *Colección Estudios CIEPLAN*, No. 11, December 1983, pp. 113-138.

5 Thoughtful discussion on the multiple origins of the debt crisis can be found in Robert Devlin, *Debt and Crisis In Latin America. The Supply Side of the Story* (Princeton: Princeton University Press, 1989); Barbara Stallings, *Banker to the Third World* (Berkeley: University of California Press, 1987); and Richard Feinberg and Valeriana Kallab, eds., *Uncertain Future: Commercial Banks and the Third World* (New Brunswick, NJ: Transaction Books for the Overseas Development Council, 1984).

6 See Patricio Rozas and Gustavo Marín, *Estado Autoritario, Deuda Externa, y Grupos Económicos* (Santiago: CESOC, Chile America, 1988).

7 Detailed information on the rising level of bankruptcies in Chile during the early 1980s is contained in Jaime Gatica Barros, *Deindustrialization in Chile* (Boulder: Westview Press, 1989), p. 38, table 2.5.

8 For a good description of the financial rescue operation, see Mauricio Larraín, "How the 1981-83 Chilean Banking Crisis Was Handled," *Working Paper*, No. 300, Policy Planning and Research Department, World Bank, December 1989.

9 See Ricardo Ffrench-Davis, *La Crisis de la Deuda Externa y el Ajuste en Chile, 1977-1986*, in Stephany Griffith-Jones, ed., *Deuda External, Renegociación y Ajuste en la America Latina* (Mexico City: Fondo de Cultura Económica, 1988), p. 125.

[10] The Chilean debt renegotiations are summarized in Ffrench-Davis, *La Crisis de la Deuda* op. cit. See also Jaime Estévez, "La Negociación Financiera Externa en Chile, 1983-1987," in Roberto Bouzas, ed., *Entre la Heterodoxie y el Ajuste: Negociaciones Financieras Externas de América Latina (1982-1987)* (Buenos Aires: Grupo Editor Latinoamericano, 1980), p. 181.

[11] The public sector guarantees extended to private debts are discussed in Ffrench-Davis, op. cit., pp. 145-149; and in Felipe Larraín, "Debt Reduction Schemes and the Management of Chilean Debt," Catholic University of Chile/Harvard University draft (mimeo.), Dec. 1988, pp. 7-8.

[12] The Central Bank of Chile has published these regulations in a bilingual circular, "Provision of the Conversion of External Debt," (not dated).

[13] D.L. 600, enacted in 1974 and revised in 1976, governs all aspects of direct foreign investment. Its revised version was published in the *Diario Oficial*, March 8, 1977, and is reprinted in Chilean Investment Committee, *Legal Framework: Chile*, appendix 9 (1988).

[14] Investors using Chapter XIX, in contrast, must provide detailed information on the source of their capital and the nature of their investment.

[15] The parallel market in Chile is a legal but unofficial market for foreign exchange transactions; its rates for exchanging Chilean pesos are slightly less favorable than those of the official market.

[16] Francisco Garcés, "La Experiencia Chilena en la capitalizacion de deuda externa, *Revista de la Federación Latinoamericana de Bancos (Revista FELABAN)*, No. 65, Aug. 1987, p. 148.

[17] Two exceptions to this are Annexes 4 and 5 to Chapter XVIII, which create special rules for conversions earmarked for recapitalizing existing enterprises or paying mortgage debts.

[18] As table 4 shows, participation in Chapter XVIII has been almost as extensive as in Chapter XIX, indicating that Chilean residents have been enthusiastic participants in debt conversions.

[19] "Chile Changes Chapter 19 Rules," *Business Latin America*, April 21, 1991, p. 131.

[20] One exception developed: by 1988, the central bank implemented a requirement that only 10 percent of large mining investments could be made through debt conversion. See J. Andrés Fontaine, "Los Mecanismos de Conversión de Deuda en Chile," *Estudios Públicos* (Oct. 1988), p. 147.

[21] The sectors in which foreign investment is limited or barred are oil, natural gas, nuclear energy, and domestic coastal shipping.

[22] As of April 1989, central bank data showed that 18 percent of Chapter XIX investments had been devoted to this sector.

[23] The procyclical behavior of Chilean stock prices is documented in Ricardo Ffrench-Davis, "Debt-Equity Swaps in Chile," *Cambridge Journal of Economics*, Vol. 14, March 1990, pp. 107-126.

24 This committee consists of the director of the national planning office; the ministers of finance, foreign affairs, and economy, development, and reconstruction; and, if an invest ment application concerns a ministry not represented on the committee, the minister of the appropriate portfolio.

25 See Felipe Larraín and Andrés Velasco, *Can Swaps Solve the Debt Crisis? Lessons from the Chilean Experience*, Princeton Studies in International Finance, No. 69 (Princeton: Dept. of Economics, Princeton University, Nov. 1990), p. 15.

26 The resulting buybacks are discussed in "Chile Buy-Back of Foreign Debt at Discount Set," *Wall Street Journal*, Sept. 22, 1988, p. 4, col. 1.

27 Several examples are discussed in F. Larraín, op.cit., p. 10.

28 Informal swaps are mostly the province of Chilean investors, however. Foreign investors prefer to use formal conversion mechanisms to obtain a right of future access to the formal foreign exchange market.

29 Two accounts of the program's origins and purposes offered by policymakers who helped to design it are Francisco Garcés, "Comentario sobre conversiones de Deuda Externa en Chile," *Boletín Mensual*, No. 710, Central Bank of Chile, April 1987, pp. 857-870; and Juan Andrés Fontaine, op. cit.

30 The potential benefits of adopting a conciliatory debt management strategy by promoting debt-equity conversions have been noted by Rudiger Dornbusch, who likened such programs to a promise that "the check is in the mail." See his comments on a paper by Jeremy Bulow and Kenneth Rogoff, "The Buyback Boondoggle," in *Brookings Papers on Economic Activity*, No. 2, 1988, p. 702.

31 "Chile wins agreement on debt rescheduling," *Financial Times*, Sept. 24, 1990, p. 2, col. 2.

32 "Chile makes successful return to world finance," *Financial Times*, Jan. 15, 1991, p. 24, col. 6.

33 See "Secondary Marketplace," *LatinFinance*, May 1991, p. 8. Chile's financial recovery is not a sure thing, however, and observers have warned that if Chile ever returns to a cycle of reschedulings and concerted lending, its debt management will be hindered by the debt conversion program, because it has reduced the proportion of its external liabilities that is renegotiable. See Ffrench-Davis, "Debt-Equity Swaps," op.cit., p. 115.

34 "Country Credit Ratings," *Institutional Investor*, Sept. 1983, p. 292, and Sept. 1989, p. 302.

35 "Getting Graded," *LatinFinance*, Dec. 1990, p. 34.

36 These figures, covering, 1985 through June 1988, were contained in an unpublished central bank study by Ivan E. Montoya, "Disposiciones Sobre Conversión de Deuda Externa en Chile: Principales Características y Resultados," August 1988. An IFC study found 100 percent additionality among investments by commercial banks via debtor-country debt-swap programs. See Joel Bergsman and Wayne Edisis, "Debt-Equity Swaps and Foreign Direct Investment in Latin America," *Discussion Paper*, #2, International Finance Corporation, 1988.

[37] One account of the motives for recent foreign investment in the forestry and paper products sectors is "Si No Puedes Vencerlos . . .," *America Economia*, No. 12, 1988, pp. 28-30. In at least one case, the central bank insisted that a foreign investor accompany its Chapter XIX investments in this sector with a significant cash contribution: New Zealand's Carter Holt Harvey purchased equity in Copec (Chile's largest private firm, which was severely weakened in the 1982 crash) with $210 million in cash. See *The Economist*, March 12, 1988, p. 95.

[38] Bergsman and Edisis, op. cit., found such a pattern.

[39] Ibid.

[40] Conversion of private debts has occurred through each of the possible formal and informal channels, but it has been most prominent in the category of direct agreements with creditors (which constitute more than half of the central bank's totals for "other" debt conversions).

[41] See "Chile's Debt-for-Equity Programme: Hotter than Most?" *International Financial Law Review*, Feb. 1990, p. 29.

[42] See "Chilean Banks Recover and Diversify," *Euromoney*, March 1988, p. 127.

[43] Ibid.

[44] Examples of the modernization and expansion projects undertaken after private sector buyouts can be found in Bergsman and Edisis, op. cit., p. 9.

[45] For example, Security Pacific is reportedly selling its investments in Latin America in an effort to consolidate operations and prepare for a merger with Bank of America. It may well sell at least some of its extensive Chilean holdings to domestic investors.

[46] The Chilean privatization program is analyzed in Mario Marcel, "La Privatización de Empresas Públicas en Chile 1985-88," *Notas Técnicas*, #125, CIEPLAN, January 1989.

[47] See "Chile Extends Popular Capitalism," *Financial Times*, June 16, 1987, p. 28, col. 4.

[48] See *Chile 1990-91*, a report of the Economist Intelligence Unit, p. 38.

[49] A final category of criticism opposes debt conversion absolutely, on the ground that it involves an unwarranted sharing of the benefits of debt relief with creditors. According to this view, debtor countries should insist on unilateral debt reductions by creditors or default on their obligations. Chile has not seriously entertained adopting such an approach, and thus its attractions and costs will not be considered here.

[50] The use of debt conversions as one element of a market-based menu approach has attracted endorsements from the leading creditor banks, the IMF and World Bank, and most Latin American debtor nations. See, for example, "Citicorp's Reed Outlines Path on Third World Loans," *The Wall Street Journal*, May 28, 1987, p. 6, col. 1; Michael Blackwell and Simon Nocera, "Debt/Equity Swaps," *IMF Working Paper*, February 12, 1988.

[51] The central bank expects that debt-conversion-related foreign exchange outflows will form a small part of a negative balance in the early 1990s, far outweighed in importance by the cost of amortizing outstanding foreign debts. See Central Bank of Chile, *Chilean External Debt 1988*, Nov. 1989, table 22.

The net effect of debt conversions on Chilean foreign exchange supplies is subject to much debate. A negative net flow will occur if, on a present-value basis, long-term dividend and capital repatriation from Chapter XIX projects is higher than the interest savings and net export earnings that these projects generate. Calculations of this net effect should also take into account the amount of cash investment displaced from D.L. 600 by Chapter XIX. See "Pagarés de la Deuda Externa: Buscando Nuevas Fórmulas," *Informes Gémines*, No. 72, Sept. 1986. Whether the final impact of conversions will be negative or positive thus depends on a number of unknowns, including the future economic environment, which will largely determine reinvestment rates for Chapter XIX investments.

[52] This point is discussed in F. Larraín, op.cit., p. 53; and in Fontaine, op.cit., p. 153.

[53] Two useful summaries and assessments of this argument are: Blackwell and Nocera, op. cit., pp. 28-31, and S. Griffith-Jones, M.S. Wionczek, K. Dezseri, and G. Marcelle, "Approaches to Third World Debt Management," *Development and Peace*, Vol. 9, No. 2, August 1988, pp. 57-58. Bergsman and Edisis, op. cit., note that only non-additional foreign investments through debt conversion exacerbate inflation.

[54] An increase in inflation in 1989-90 may have resulted in part from the pressures of high levels of debt conversion, although accelerated public spending before the 1989 presidential election also contributed to the problem. For a further discussion of the difficulty of fully sterilizing the inflationary consequences of debt conversions, see the comments by Joaquín Vial on this essay.

[55] A good study of the rebirth of Chile's private financial sector is F. Larraín, op. cit.

[56] These costs are at the heart of criticisms made in Larraín and Velasco, op. cit.

[57] See, for example, Ffrench-Davis, "Debt-Equity Swaps," op. cit.

[58] Ibid.

[59] Central bank data.

[60] Monthly secondary market price surveys, *LatinFinance*.

[61] According to central bank data, only $417 million in debt was converted through Chapter XIX in 1990, compared to a total of $1.3 billion for 1989.

[62] Data are from Central Bank of Chile, *Economic and Financial Report*, Aug. 1990, table 31.

[63] See "Secondary Market Survey," *LatinFinance*, March 1991, p. 66.

[64] See, for example, John F.H. Purcell, Joyce Chang, and Dirk W. Damrau, *Chile: An Investment-Grade Credit*, a remarkably upbeat report by the Sovereign Assessment Group at Salomon Brothers, May 1991.

[65] Roberto Bouzas and Saúl Keifman, "El 'Menú de Opciones' y El Programa de Capitalización de la Deuda Externa Argentina," in Bouzas and Ffrench-Davis, op. cit., p. 30. Much of the chronology and detail presented here on Argentina's debt conversions is drawn from this article and from a draft paper by Michael Mortimore, "Debt Equity Conversions: From Promoting Foreign Investment to Capturing the Discount," prepared for the U.N. CEPAL/CET Joint Unit, Santiago, Chile, Spring 1991.

[66] Nathaniel C. Nash, "Vital Signs Quickening in Argentina," *The New York Times*, August 27, 1991, p. D-1, col. 6.

[67] See Bouzas and Keifman, op.cit., p. 39, table 3.

[68] Bouzas and Keifman, op. cit., elaborate on these costs of the Argentine debt conversion program.

[69] "Completed Latin American Privatization Transactions in 1990-91" (table), *LatinFinance*, June 1991, p. 42.

[70] "Iberia, Argentine Government in Dispute Over Aerolineas Payments," *Aviation Daily*, Vol. 305, No. 12, July 18, 1991, p. 110.

[71] "Secondary Marketplace," *LatinFinance*, April 1991, p. 14.

[72] This program is briefly described in Mortimore, op. cit., pp. 31-32.

[73] The political pressures favoring conversions are described in Francisco Eduardo Pires de Souza, "Conversión de la Deuda Externa en Inversión Directa: Una Evaluación de la Experiencia Brasile:a Reciente," in Bouzas and Ffrench-Davis, op. cit., p. 65.

[74] See the section on Brazilian debt conversions in U.N. Centre on Transnational Corporations, *Debt Equity Conversions: A Guide for Decision-Makers* (New York, 1990), p. 72.

[75] Mortimore, op. cit., p. 32.

[76] Pires de Souza, op. cit., p. 60.

[77] Ibid.

[78] "Banks' Brazil Committee Mulls Counterproposal," *LDC Debt Report/Latin American Markets*, Vol. 4, No. 33, Sept. 16, 1991, p.1.

[79] "Brazil," *LDC Debt Report/Latin American Markets*, Vol. 4, No. 18, May 20, 1991, p. 9.

[80] See Victor M. Godínez and Inder J. Ruprah, "En Busca del Descuento del Mercado: México y El Enfoque no Convencional de la Deuda Externa," in Bouzas and Ffrench-Davis, op.cit., p. 160. Further information on Mexico's conversion programs is drawn from Mortimore, *op. cit.*

[81] Godínez and Ruprah, op. cit., p. 158.

[82] José Manuel Surez-Mier, "Mexico's Debt Strategy," *The Journal of International Securities Markets*, Autumn 1989, p. 256.

[83] Mortimore, op. cit., p. 22.

[84] One recent report suggests that Mexico's debt to private banks has dropped at least 20 percent since 1982. Ibid., p. 21.

[85] "How Debt-Equity Swaps Are Used in Privatization," *Business Latin America*, Nov. 19, 1990, p. 379.

[86] For a cautiously optimistic article on ongoing capital market development in Mexico, see Timothy Heyman, "Euphoria on Reforma," *LatinFinance*, June 1991, p. 31.

[88] "Mexico's Debt to Rise in Post Debt Relief World," *LDC Debt Report/Latin American Reports*, Vol. 4, No. 4, Feb. 4, 1991, p. 3.

Comments on

Debt Conversion Programs in Latin America

. . . .

COMMENTARY BY LAWRENCE J. BRAINARD

■ AS MARY WILLIAMSON NOTES in her introduction, debt conversions are widely viewed as a vital tool for overcoming the Latin American debt crisis. I would argue that the prevailing conceptual model that leads to such a conclusion is flawed. Nonetheless, debt conversions can contribute to economic stabilization provided they are consistent with a balanced fiscal policy.

The traditional view of debt conversions is that they strengthen a country's creditworthiness by reducing the outflow of foreign exchange associated with the servicing of foreign debt. This "balance-of-payments" approach is based on tracing the source of the debt crisis to a shortage of foreign exchange to meet scheduled debt servicing requirements.

Perhaps the best illustration of the pervasive influence of this model in thinking about possible solutions to the debt crisis is found in the official debt strategy for developing country debt. Since the beginning of the debt crisis in 1982, the Group of Seven finance ministers have regularly endorsed an explicit strategy for dealing with the debt, which was implemented in cooperation with the multilateral financial institutions such as the International Monetary Fund and the World Bank.

In 1982, Treasury Secretary Donald Regan introduced the Treasury's five-point program as the basis for the official strategy; the program highlighted the important role of "new money" from commercial banks.

Official efforts placed top priority on the negotiation of such new-money packages for all reschedulings in major debtor countries during 1982-83.

The original Treasury program faltered, and a revised debt strategy was formulated and introduced by Regan's successor, James Baker, in October 1985. The earlier focus on new money was maintained; the Baker Plan for resolving the debt crisis made new money the linchpin of the official debt strategy. The plan targeted $29 billion in net additional financing—$20 billion from commercial banks and $9 billion from multilateral development banks—for a list of fifteen major debtor countries during 1986-88, over and above a sum of $11 billion already planned for the period.

In March 1989, Treasury Secretary Nicholas Brady abandoned the Baker Plan by shifting the focus of the official debt strategy to debt reduction. In view of the lack of meaningful success associated with the official strategy during the 1980s, it is pertinent to ask why the new-money approach fared so poorly.

The primary flaw of the balance-of-payments approach to solving the debt crisis is that it ignores the fiscal relationship between the private sector and the government. In the majority of debtor countries, the bulk of foreign debt is owed by the government, but most foreign exchange is earned by the private sector.[1] To service its debt, the government must purchase the needed foreign exchange from the private sector, paying with domestic monetary resources. The fundamental issue concerns how the government obtains the needed domestic resources in the first place.

One option is for the government to balance its budget by reprogramming expenditures and revenues and reforming budgetary policies. Other alternatives include increasing domestic government borrowing, hiking the pace of monetary emission, and similar methods of confiscating private savings. The official debt strategy sought to provide financing of government deficits by means of forced loans from foreign creditors. The fallacy of this approach was that it viewed the debt crisis primarily as a balance-of-payments difficulty rather than a fiscal problem.

The balanced budget option is the only strategy that gives the state the needed resources without undermining private-sector confidence in the government. Increased borrowing by the government from either domestic or foreign creditors cannot improve confidence, given the existing uncertainty about the government's ability to meet its obligations. This lack of confidence finds reflection in continued high real rates of interest on domestic government debt, capital flight, and reduced inflows of foreign investment. These factors frustrate efforts to restore economic growth and investment and undermine attempts to implement sound fiscal policies.

The official debt strategy had the unintended result of persuading governments that a lesser fiscal adjustment effort was enough, given the availability of new-money from the banks. In fact, a more radical fiscal restructuring was called for, including tax reform, elimination of subsidies, and large-scale privatization of state-owned firms.

In 1987 two Mexican economists working at the International Monetary Fund, Alain Ize and Guillermo Ortiz, published research that for the first time provided a plausible explanation for the failure of the new-money strategy.[2] Their theoretical model, based on Mexican experience since 1982, introduced a new perspective by viewing debt problems from within a fiscal framework. They presented a model of government fiscal performance and the reactions of domestic investors in government paper to such behavior. Ize and Ortiz identify the close linkage between domestic and foreign debt, which affects the fiscal budget through changes in private-sector confidence in the ability of the state to service its debt.

The fiscal perspective contributed by Ize and Ortiz provides the appropriate analytical framework for assessing the potential contribution of debt conversions to a solution of the debt crisis. Thus, if debt conversions contribute to a worsening of the state's fiscal position, its ability to service its total debt (both external and internal) is weakened. This is likely to be the case for official programs tied to private-sector conversions of public debt.

On the other hand, official debt conversion programs tied to privatizations are likely to strengthen the government's fiscal position, because in privatizing the state is often getting rid of loss-making enterprises that drained resources from the government budget. Argentina's current privatization program has already helped to restore a significant degree of confidence in public finances simply because many of the white elephants being sold will no longer be a burden for the fiscal accounts.

It may be argued that debt conversion programs are unnecessary for the success of privatizations, because state firms could always be sold for cash rather than discounted debt. This view neglects the dynamics of the debt renegotiating process. The most important contribution of debt conversions, in my view, is to provide the state with a negotiating lever in debt reduction discussions with the creditor banks.

At the same time, linking privatizations to reductions in the government's domestic debt could provide the same boost to private-sector confidence that foreign debt-equity conversions have contributed. So long as an emphasis is placed on maintaining fiscal balance when implementing debt conversions, Latin American debtors should experiment with this variation on the debt conversion theme.

The Chilean experience illustrates a final constructive approach to harmonizing debt conversions with fiscal balance. As Table 4 of Williamson's essay highlights, informal debt conversions have accounted for almost one-third of the overall foreign debt reduction that Chile has achieved. Informal transactions involving private debts do not require any public expenditures or guarantees and thus provide an incentive to private investment without threatening the fiscal balance.

As Williamson notes in her conclusion, the contribution of debt conversions depends importantly on the "overall coherence and stability" of a country's economic program. Given a suitable context, debt conversions have a definite contribution to make. Most important, though, is for countries to create the appropriate conditions by first addressing the fiscal issues that lie at the heart of the debt crisis.

Notes

1 Venezuela and Nigeria are exceptions, as the bulk of export earnings derive from sales of petroleum products by state-owned companies—80 percent in Venezuela and 96 percent in Nigeria. Mexico's oil exports account for only 37 percent of total exports.

2 Alain Ize and Guillermo Ortiz, "Fiscal Rigidities, Public Debt, and Capital Flight," *Staff Papers*, International Monetary Fund, Vol. 34, June 1987, pp. 311-322.

COMMENTARY BY JOAQUÍN VIAL

■   MARY WILLIAMSON OFFERS A VERY CAREFUL discussion of debt conversion programs, presenting a well-informed and balanced view of the issues. This is remarkable in a field in which opinions are heavily loaded by ideological preconceptions and special interests.

The main contributions of the essay are the thorough review of several countries actual experiences with debt conversion mechanisms and the policy lessons extracted from these case studies. I fully agree with Williamson's conclusion that debt conversions "are neither the cure nor the curse that some observers have claimed." Debt conversion programs are not an end in themselves, and their costs and benefits should be weighted through careful consideration of the specifics of each country's situation and the overall coherence of its economic policies.

Williamson argues strongly for "coherent economic policies to back debt conversion programs." I endorse this point of view, although I do not think Chile was as successful in this respect as she maintains. In any case, this is a key element for the design of debt conversion programs, especially when the countries face rampant inflation. I also agree that debt conversion programs have a limited future, once the country enters a recovery phase and debt service becomes manageable. The very success of debt conversions will cause their end, as prices in the secondary market edge upward.

I will confine my comments to three specific issues surrounding the Chilean experience with debt conversion. First, I want to address the impact of debt conversion on domestic financial markets. Second, I will refer to the contribution of debt conversion programs to the recovery of the Chilean economy. Finally, I will comment on the costs and benefits of the conversion mechanisms.

DEBT CONVERSION AND
DOMESTIC FINANCIAL MARKETS

As Williamson explains, whenever there is a debt conversion operation, money creation occurs, unless the central bank replaces the amount of foreign debt converted with domestic debt. If the domestic market is not deep or sophisticated enough, or if the domestic national debt is already too high, the central bank will not be able to sell the debt on the domestic market, or interest rates will go up, crowding out private expenditure, with negative effects on investment. This was one of the main reasons why debt conversions in Mexico had a bad start. After reviewing the Chilean experience, the author concludes that "debt conversions can be structured to neutralize their monetary effects as Chile has successfully done," notwithstanding some crowding out of private investment and some pressure on interest rates.

Inflation in Chile remained relatively low and stable during the second half of the 1980s, with a low of 12.7 percent in 1988 and a peak of 27.3 percent in 1990. These rates are low, not only by Southern Cone standards but also compared with Chile's recent history. However, this comparison is deceptive: I am convinced that in the mid-1980s Chile was in a position to reduce the "natural rate of inflation" from 20-25 percent to a rate between 10 and 15 percent. One of the reasons why this did not happen was the big expansion in money supply between the second half of 1987 and the third quarter of 1988.

At that time the central bank was setting the interest rate for key central bank papers and providing all the liquidity "demanded" by the market at that rate. Debt conversion operations put pressure on the domestic financial market, but it did not show up in interest rates, which were (indirectly) controlled by the central bank, but on money supply. The expansion in liquidity (60 percent in annual terms at its peak in October 1988) had a delayed impact on inflation, partly due to specific actions by the government (VAT rate reduction, import tariffs, cuts, etc.) in the face of the upcoming referendum on the Pinochet government, and also because of the natural lag in price responses.[1] Monetary policy was tightened after the referendum, and real interest rates were allowed to rise from 4.6 percent (annual average for 1988) to 8.9 percent at the end of 1989.

Therefore, I would conclude that massive debt conversions, like those undertaken in Chile, definitely have a significant impact in domestic markets. If the central bank has an interest rate target, the money supply will increase and inflationary pressures will arise.[2] If the central bank has a quantitative target for its monetary policy, then interest rates will rise, with a negative impact on private consumption and investment. The existence of deep and well-developed financial markets is a precondition for reaching the targets of monetary policy, but it does not eliminate the costs of debt conversions.

DEBT CONVERSION
AND THE BUSINESS CLIMATE

Williamson rightly asserts that one of the key contributions of the debt conversion programs was their promotion of a favorable climate for foreign investment in Chile. However, their is another aspect in which these programs had a positive effect: they helped to bolster domestic business confidence, which had been shaken to the core by the exchange and financial crises of the early 1980s. Private investment fell to its lowest levels since the socialist experiment of President Allende. The recovery of the economy in the mid-1980s, as well as the increase in public investment, was not enough to induce new investment by the private sector. Debt conversions helped to change this situation in two ways: they provided a cheap and easy way to recapitalize overindebted companies, and the inflow of foreign investment had a demonstration effect on the local business community.

I am convinced that this positive contribution is usually understated. However, its usefulness is limited only to the early stages of the recovery process, when a "big push" is needed to revitalize the economy.

DEBT CONVERSION MECHANISMS IN CHILE

Williamson's description and analysis of debt conversion mechanisms is complete, and I generally agree with her assessment. There are, however, a couple of additional points I would like to make. First, there is a rather negative depiction of the "informal" debt conversion operations. Although most of these operations had a shaky legal bases,[3] they had a rather positive impact from an economic point of view: they not only extinguished all foreign obligations without monetary or fiscal impacts, but debtors were able to obtain very large discounts, especially during the first years, when many foreign banks opted to absorb significant losses in loans to private companies in Chile. One of the costs of the execution of the public sector guarantee of loans to private banks was that it discouraged many banks from accepting major losses in debt conversion operations.

The author rightly mentions that many problems in the application of debt conversion operations were gradually corrected. Key among them were the discrimination in favor of foreign investors implicit in Chapter XIX and the problems of additionality and selectivity of investment. However, it is worth mentioning that most of the corrections were introduced in 1989 or 1990—after most of the debt conversions had already taken place. A major cost of the delay in carrying out these corrections was the unfair advantage given to foreign investors in the bid for state enterprises offered for sale as part of the privatization program.

A final point is that programs like these, which have the potential to channel massive subsidies without a direct and evident fiscal cost, can degenerate into a system for "rent distribution." One example of this type of behavior was the use of Chapter XVIII to compensate fruit farmers after the episode of "grape poisoning" in the United States in 1988. After that, several proposals arose for "compensating" different interest groups. Fortunately, most of them were not implemented. This is one of the reasons why a debt reduction program should be carried out in a less discretionary framework than in Chile.

Notes

[1] The official explanation for these policies can be found in Juan Andrés Fontaine, "La administración de la politica monetaria en Chile, 1985-89," *Cuadernos de Economía*, No. 83, April 1991. A different interpretation of the events can be found in Daniel Tapia, "Dos pruebas para la política monetaria," *Cuadernos de Economía*, No. 83.

[2] There is significant evidence that the money supply has a direct effect on private expenditure, in addition to any indirect effects through interest rates. See Sergio Lehman "Sensibilidad de la inversion productiva y del consumo del sector privado ante variaciones de la tasa de interés real" M.A. thesis, University of Chile, 1991.

[3] They are perfectly legal under the central bank's Organic Law, in effect since the end of 1989.

About the Authors

MARY L. WILLIAMSON was a Program Assistant at the Overseas Development Council from 1985-87 and has also worked for the World Bank, the Overseas Private Investment Corporation, the Multilateral Investment Guarantee Agency, as well as at private law firms in Seattle and Washington, D.C. Her publications include "The Role of Banking Regulations in Third World Debt Strategies," *ODC Working Paper* (1988); "What Can Be Done to Stem Latin America's Money Exodus?" (with Richard E. Feinberg); *Directors and Boards* (1987); and "Moving the World Bank's MIGA Forward," *Journal of Commerce* (1986).

LAWRENCE J. BRAINARD is Vice President and Director of Research of the Emerging Debt Markets Group of Goldman, Sachs, & Co. Until the end of 1990 he was head of international economic and political analysis at Bankers Trust Company. Since the mid-1980s, Mr. Brainard has been actively involved with working out problems associated with the international indebtedness of developing countries. He has participated as a member of economic committees established by creditor banks to evaluate economic developments associated with debt reschedulings in Poland, Yugoslavia, Nigeria, Brazil, and Mexico. His essay "Reform in Eastern Europe: Creating a Capital Market," was awarded the first prize in the 1990 Amex Bank Review awards.

JOAQUÍN VIAL is an economist and full time researcher at the Corporacion de Investigaciones Economicas para América Latina (CIEPLAN) in Santiago, Chile. Currently, he heads CIEPLAN's research team in macroeconomics. His main areas of research include international economics, macroeconomics, and analysis of commodity markets. Before joining CIEPLAN in 1988, he worked for the University of Chile and the University of Santiago.

About the ODC

The Overseas Development Council's programs focus on U.S. relations with developing countries in five broad policy areas: U.S. foreign policy and developing countries in a post-Cold War era; international finance and easing the debt crisis; international trade during the Uruguay Round, and beyond; development strategies and development cooperation; and environment and development.

Within these major policy themes, ODC seeks to increase American understanding of the economic and social problems confronting the developing countries and to promote awareness of the importance of these countries to the United States in an increasingly interdependent international system. In pursuit of these goals, ODC functions as:

■ A center for policy analysis. Bridging the worlds of ideas and actions, ODC translates the best academic research and analysis on selected issues of policy importance into information and recommendations for policymakers in the public and private sectors.

■ A forum for the exchange of ideas. ODC's conferences, seminars, workshops, and briefings brings together legislators, business executives, scholars, and representatives of international financial institutions and non-governmental groups.

■ A resource for public education. Through its publications, meetings, testimony, lectures, and formal and informal networking, ODC makes timely, objective, non-partisan information available to an audience that includes but reaches far beyond the Washington policymaking community.

Board of Directors

Overseas Development Council
SPECIAL PUBLICATIONS SUBSCRIPTION OFFER

U.S.-Third World Policy Perspectives

Policy Essays • Policy Focus

As a subscriber to the ODC's three publications series, you will have access to an invaluable source of independent analyses of U.S.-Third World issues—economic, political, and social—at a savings of 30 percent off the regular price.

■ Brief and easy-to-read, each **Policy Focus** briefing paper provides background information and analysis on a current topic on the policy agenda. In 1992, 8-10 papers will cover aspects of U.S. trade, aid, finance, and security policy toward the developing countries.

■ **Policy Essays** explore critical issues on the U.S.-Third World agenda in 60-80 succinct pages, offering concrete recommendations for action. In 1992, a special five-part "conditionality series" will explore the potential utility and the limits of attaching conditions to aid, trade, and technology transfers to encourage sustained changes in certain policies and behavior of other governments. A separate essay will explore the North-South environmental strategies, costs, and bargains to be raised at the U.N. Conference on Environment and Development.

■ **U.S.-Third World Policy Perspectives,** ODC's policy book series, brings a wide range of expertise to bear on current issues facing American policymakers. Each volume presents creative new policy options or insights into the implications of existing policy. *Free Trade Fever: U.S.-Latin American Trade Relations in the 1990s* will be released in mid-1992.

SUBSCRIPTION OPTIONS

Special Publications Subscription Offer*	$65.00
(All U.S.-Third World Policy Perspectives (1), Policy Essays (5-6), and Policy Focus briefing papers (8-10) issued in 1992.)	
1992 Policy Focus Subscription Offer*	$20.00
(Foreign)	$19.00
Individual Titles	
U.S.-Third World Policy Perspectives	$15.95
Policy Essay	$9.95

* Subscribers will receive all 1992 publications issued to date upon receipt of payment; other publications will be sent upon release. Book-rate postage is included in price.

All orders require prepayment. For individual titles, add $1.00 per item for shipping and handling. Please send check or money order to:

Publication Orders
Overseas Development Council
1717 Massachusetts Avenue, NW
Suite 501
Washington, DC 20036

O | D | C